SNATCHED FROM THE FIRE

A Young Woman's Life Consumed By Darkness

A Testimony by Prophetess Patricia Amis

authorHOUSE®

AuthorHouse™
1663 Liberty Drive, Suite 200
Bloomington, IN 47403
www.authorhouse.com
Phone: 1-800-839-8640

First published by AuthorHouse 11/12/2007

ISBN: 978-1-4343-3606-4 (sc)

Library of Congress Control Number: 2007907495

Printed in the United States of America
Bloomington, Indiana

This book is printed on acid-free paper.

ACKNOWLEDGMENTS

I would like to first thank my heavenly father for allowing me to know who he is, and what he represents. I am also thankful for the creator of our universe who allowed his Holy Spirit to overshadow my life, which set me free. I am thankful that JESUS CHRIST died for our sins so that we may have a right to the tree of life. I would like to also give thanks to my mother, Rachel Smith, who experienced many sleepless nights while praying for me; Aunt Doris Smith (AKA "Billie Jean") who always stepped in when I needed her; my sister Denise Smith, who fought many battles for me when I didn't even know it; my beautiful, intelligent daughter, Rachel Fenton, and my handsome son, Steve Fenton Jr., who always stayed by my side and believed in me, even when it seemed as if I had given up on hope.

I would like to express a royal Thank You to my husband Reginald who is my best friend, who remained supportive while I finished this project.

Many more thanks to all of my associates in the universe. Words could never describe how much I appreciate all of your support, so I will sum it up and say "I love you."

Foreword

Just because we cannot see it, does not mean that it will not affect us. Danger always resides within the darkness, when there is no light present in order to manifest hope. Sometimes we make decisions not realizing that there exists a lurking, dangerous fire that you become a part of and that commands to be a part of you. Some people notice the fire in your life, and dare not to expose it. The individuals who have no knowledge concerning the mystery of the camouflages are seated in the safety zone of life. No matter where you run or where you hide, the fire finds you. Once you decide that you do not want to be a part of this dangerous fire, it decides not to take "no" for an answer. The fire will affect every area of your life adversely, once you reject it. Sabrina never knew that the fire was real. She never detected the camouflage that was presented before her. She never believed in the path regarding the truth that sets individuals free. Sabrina became a part of the fire, and is snatched away into a marvelous light of freedom by a man that she always dreamed about . . .

SNATCHED FROM THE FIRE

It was the year 1989. I was a sophomore, attending Wagner College. I was very happy at the time, because within two more years I would be graduating from college. I was also elated because I had a wardrobe that everyone admired, and I was the perfect role model in college. Writing papers all day, quoting Shakespeare and visiting the library were starting to bore me. On one cold winter day I decided to take a break from my studies and go for a ride on the Staten Island Ferry. As I sat down on my seat, I noticed a young man seated across from me. He was quite attractive, tall and had a distinctive gleam in his eyes. He was accompanied by a little boy and girl. I felt the urge to speak to him. Finally, I got up enough courage and spoke to the young man.

"Hello," my name is Sabrina.

"Hi," he said, "my name is Keno. Are you from Brooklyn?"

"No," I replied. "I'm a Staten Island girl." We both chuckled. He proceeded to introduce the little boy.

"This is my younger brother. His name is Johnny. He is nine years old. This is my sister Sandra. She is seven years old."

The two youngsters appeared quite friendly. We exchanged numbers and I promised Keno that I would call him. A week later I called Keno. On that particular day, Keno invited me out to dinner. At first, I was ashamed to give him my address, because I lived in the Stapleton Projects. Stapleton was one of the primary ghettos of Staten Island. This was a place where many individuals had to literally fight in order to survive. This was a place where you either allow the beast to rule you, or you found enough courage to establish a game of survival. I figured that I had nothing to lose. I finally gave Keno my address.

"Fine," stated Keno, "I will pick you up on Friday at 8:00 p.m."

I was so excited. On Friday night, Keno picked me up for our dinner date. I could not help but notice the same gleam that appeared in his eyes when I first met him.

"Hi," exclaimed Keno as I sat down into the vehicle.

I replied "Hello."

This was, in fact, the first time that I actually went on a genuine date. As we drove down the streets of Staten Island, I could not help but notice the neighborhoods that we passed. There were all beautiful homes with manicured lawns, scenery that I was generally quite unfamiliar with.

"So how long have you been living on Staten Island?" asked Keno.

"I actually grew up on Staten Island," I cheerfully replied.

"Interesting, Sabrina," Keno replied. "I have been living on Staten Island for five years. I'm originally from New Jersey. I live in my parents' home, in the Mariners Harbor section of the island. I am a part time college student, and I work full time for a New York City agency."

As he finished his sentence, we pulled up into the driveway of a well-known restaurant. "WINDOWS ON WONDERS" read the awning above the restaurant. As I looked up, I could not help but notice the tapered-glossy windows of the restaurant, along with the gleaming lights, which appeared magical. We entered into the restaurant and there were freshly picked flowers, and a dimly-lit candle on each table. The entire room was also lit dimly. I noticed the reflection of the candle lights move slowly across Keno's handsome face. I could feel my mind literally racing, hoping that the evening would turn out perfect.

As the waiter sat us at the table, I asked Keno to excuse me, while I went to the ladies room. When I entered the ladies room I noticed a mirror on the wall encircled by the brightest bubble lights that I have ever seen! As I looked into the mirror and saw the bright reflection of my face, I heard a familiar voice of a female speak to me. She said, "Be yourself. If you are yourself, he will get to know you. If you pretend to be someone else, he will not get to know you. Relax and let the evening flow naturally." As I looked away from the mirror, I felt a strong urgency to return back to the table in order to accompany Keno.

When I arrived back at the table the waiter had already placed two glasses of iced water and a basket of hot bread in the center of the table. Keno and I ordered our food. We were enjoying each other's conversation during the meal. At the end of the evening, Keno dropped me off in the front of my building. "181 GORDON STREET" read the bold-lettered sign on the front of the project building where I resided. As I opened the car door in order to get out, I noticed about fifteen men who appeared to be in their mid-twenties jogging in line. They appeared quite disciplined. The men resembled soldiers training for war. They all had serious looks on their faces, and had bodies of steel. This was not the first time that I'd seen these young men around the neighborhood. I was informed in the past that they were the famous Paris Crew who lived in the Stapleton Projects where I resided. Although I had heard about all of the other neighborhoods that they had conquered, I was not afraid. They never bothered me.

"Good night," stated Keno.

"Good night," I replied.

"I will call you tomorrow," exclaimed Keno.

I shut the door to Keno's vehicle and watched him fade away into the evening sunset.

Eight months had already passed by, and Keno and I were getting to know each other by spending a lot of quality time together, talking, going to the movies, and enjoying intimate times together. As far as I was concerned, Keno was my king. There was nothing that I would not do in order to keep him by my side. I started to feel like Keno was all that I had, ever had, and ever would have. I felt as if I were mysteriously falling in love with Keno. I always looked forward to spending time with him.

It was a bright sunny day, when I visited Keno at his parents' home. I could feel the warm, hot sun beaming down on my freshly-crimped hair. I could smell the illuminating smell of newly-lit charcoal in the air. The children on Keno's block were cheerfully playing in the middle of the street. As I entered Keno's residence, Keno's mother, Ms. Williams, was in the kitchen preparing a meal.

"Hello, Sabrina."

"Hello," I exclaimed in a soft, monotone voice.

She was a fair-skinned woman in her mid-forties with locks in her hair. She seemed quite happy with her profession as a registered nurse. I sat in the chair while Ms. Williams was seasoning her stew while standing. Well, I had known Ms. Williams for at least eight months now. She had been divorced from Mr. Williams for three years. I have never seen her in the company of a man since I had been visiting.

I often saw a particular female visit Ms. Williams. She seemed a little older than Ms. Williams.

"Well, you and Keno seem to be getting along just fine, Sabrina."

"Yes," I replied, "Keno makes me very happy and I finally feel like my life is completed."

"That is very good," replied Ms. Williams. "Oh, by the way, Sabrina, if you don't mind, I will need you to baby-sit little John and Sandra, maybe every evening from now on, until further notice."

Well, Ms. Williams was a bold soul with words.

"I may need you to cook for them, make sure that their hair is combed and make sure that they are ready for school on the next day. Perhaps you may need to move in."

"Well," I replied, "that doesn't seem like a bad idea. It beats staying home, living in a cramped room without Keno."

"I have already discussed the situation with Keno, and he was fine with the idea."

"Fine," I replied. Besides, my classes were in the morning. "I will gather my belongings together, and have Keno bring them over."

Abruptly, Ms. Williams leaned over and whispered in my ear. "I must confess, Sabrina, the female that you see visiting me often, that is my lover. Her name is Rosa. I am gay."

Before I was able to respond, I noticed that Keno had been in the living room listening to our conversation.

"Oh my goodness," Keno exclaimed, "my mother is gay."

Keno proceeded to run up the stairs. Ms. Williams and I proceeded to run after him. Keno slammed his bedroom door.

"I need to speak to Sabrina alone. Mom, do not come in here" he yelled as he stood behind the locked bedroom door. Finally, Ms.

Williams hastily walked downstairs, and Keno opened the door with his eyes bloodshot red, filled with tears.

"I am sorry," I exclaimed. I was brought up in a Christian home where we were taught that men should be with women, and women with men. Either way, I would not discriminate. I am not one to judge. People do what they do.

" I never knew that my mother was gay," exclaimed Keno. "She never told me. Why? How could she do this?"

"Well, Keno, that is a question that you will need to ask your mother. I am certain that your mother did not intend to hurt you. Everything will be fine, Keno," I stated as I hugged Keno and wiped the tears from his bloodshot eyes. "Remember, Keno, I am here for you. It will be okay."

"Thank you," replied Keno. "Later on I will drive you to your home so that you can pick up your belongings."

"Fine," I replied as I walked downstairs into the cold, dreary living room. I thought to myself, "How am I going to tell my mother that I'm moving out, into Keno's home?" My mother was a very old fashioned Christian woman. I wondered how I was going to convince her that this would be the best decision for me.

Keno had just returned from the corner store. "Okay, Sabrina, I am ready to drive you to your mother's home so that you can pick up your clothing." As we were driving along the ritzy neighborhoods of the island, Keno was staring blankly into the rear view mirror of the car. For some strange reason the ride to my mother's house seemed longer than usual.

"Bye, Keno," I stated as I opened the car door of his vehicle.

"I will meet you later, at my mother's house," replied Keno.

I hastily ran to my building, got into the elevator, and pressed the #7 button. When the elevator door opened, I ran to apartment 7C and knocked on the front door. My mother opened the door with a shrewd smile on her face.

"Hello, Sabrina, how are you today?"

"Fine, Mom. I need to talk to you about Keno. His mother told me that she is gay. Keno overheard her telling me, and he is very upset about the situation. He did not take it too well," I exclaimed. I could not get up enough courage to tell my mother that I was moving out, into Keno's house. After all, my mother was no fool.

"Mom, I need to stay over Keno's house for a few days out of the week. I am not actually moving in, but I will be assisting Ms. Williams with the kids until she settles a situation that she is dealing with at this time."

"Sabrina, you know how I feel about one spending nights with a mate before marriage, but if you believe that this is the right decision for your life, you are free to go."

Wow, I was expecting my mother to hit the roof, especially since she had met Keno in person only five times within the past five months. She always spoke kindly to him over the telephone when he called in order to speak to me, and vice versa. Perhaps my mother finally realized that I was getting older. Besides, she had my sister who is two years younger than me. She always kept my mother company. My father had never lived with us, so my mother must have subconsciously accepted my quest for a dominant father figure in my life. I began to calmly pack some of my clothing into the suitcase.

Over time, staying over Keno's house for a few days out of the week turned into weeks at a time. I found myself struggling to stay on top of my studies. I was beginning to feel like the live-in maid. I was cooking, shopping, and cleaning for Keno and his younger siblings, while Ms. Williams disappeared on her rendezvous with her lover, Rosa.

It had been three months since I had been living with Keno and his family. One cold morning when I woke up, the house seemed very dreary and cold. I glanced at the clock, and it read 6:00 a.m. I got out of the bed and looked for Keno, but he was no place to be found. I walked downstairs into the kitchen, then into the living room, and nobody was there. I found that to be quite unusual, since someone was always at home during the morning. I looked into John and Sandra's room and it was empty. I looked into Ms. Williams' room, and it was also empty. I proceeded to go back upstairs into Keno's room—the room that we shared. As I opened the door to the bathroom, an automatic light switched on, and on the mirror was written in red lipstick—SABRINA WILL YOU MARRY ME? An arrow was pointed downward. I proceeded to move slowly, closer towards the sink. Inside the sink, under the pointed arrow was a box. I abruptly opened the box, and there it was—a beautiful diamond engagement ring. It was the most beautiful diamond that I had ever seen!! I screamed in a loud voice, and began to cry.

I began to exclaim, "Yes, Keno, I will marry you."

I immediately put the ring onto my finger, vowing never to take it off. I hastily ran into the bedroom and called my mother. I was so excited!!

"Hello," exclaimed my mother.

"Hi, mom, this is Sabrina," I stated breathlessly. "Keno just proposed to me. He left the ring in a box inside of the sink. He wrote in red lipstick on the mirror, "Would you marry me?" I was talking so fast that I could hardly speak clearly.

"Oh, dear daughter, congratulations," exclaimed my mother. "I'm very happy for the both of you. I really hope that everything works out well for the both of you."

"Thanks, mom. I am so happy."

"Well, Sabrina, where is Keno?"

"When I woke up early this morning, he was not here. Actually, mom, nobody was home at all. I am so excited about the plans that I have to make regarding our wedding. Don't you remember, mom, that peach and grey are my favorite colors? Those are the colors that I am going to pick for the wedding. As soon as Keno and I pick a wedding date, I will inform the rest of the family regarding our engagement. Tell my sister Dana the good news. I am certain that she will be excited." Well, my sister Dana was not very fond of Keno. She just tolerated him because I tolerated her friends. I guess that the old saying is true. One hand washes the other and they both wash your face.

"Okay, Sabrina," replied my mother. "I will speak to you later. You two be good to each other."

"Okay, goodbye," I said. I immediately rushed back into the bathroom and took a nice, warm shower. I must have been in the shower for at least twenty minutes, or so. When I got out of the shower, Keno was sitting on the bed, dressed in a white tuxedo, holding a bouquet of roses. I abruptly ran over to him, wrapped in my towel, and said, "Yes, I will marry you."

"I love you, Sabrina," stated Keno.

I replied, "I love you too."

Keno began to softly kiss my lips. Keno abruptly interrupted our intimate moment when he exclaimed, "Sabrina, get dressed." Keno slowly opened the closet. There it was—the most beautiful peach-colored satin gown that I have ever seen!!!

Keno said, "Sabrina, try it on." The gown was satin-peach with white roses around the waist. The thin, white straps casually hung off of my shoulders. There was a sexy slit that accented the left side of my thigh. I was dressed to kill. I fixed my hair in a French roll, put on my black patent leather pumps, and we were ready to go.

"Oh, Keno, by the way—where are we going?" I asked with a shrewd smile.

"Just step outside, my sweetheart Sabrina, and you will see for yourself." As I slowly opened the front door of the house, I noticed that there was a white stretched limousine parked in the driveway.

"Oh, no, you didn't," I shouted in a loud monotone voice.

"Yes, I did," shouted Keno.

"Come on, Keno, let's go." We hastily got into the ritzy limousine. The old-fashioned digital clock read 11:30 a.m. There were two bottles of Moet champagne chilling over a bucket of ice.

"Oh, Keno, this is so romantic!! This is so beautiful. I do not know what else to say. You made me so happy. I want to spend the rest of my life with you."

"You are very special to me, Sabrina. I don't ever want to lose you. I love you, baby girl."

Keno and I had lunch at a beautiful restaurant by the seaside. We spent hours riding around town in the limousine drinking champagne, and listening to music.

"This has been a day to remember," stated Keno. The clock in the limousine read 6 o'clock p.m. It was time to go home. The limousine driver dropped us off at home. The day was over. The memories would always be unforgettable.

Today was my day!! I called my best friend Sheba and gave her the good news.

"Hello, Sheba, this is Sabrina."

"Hi, Sabrina."

"I am calling you in order to tell you that Keno and I have gotten engaged. We don't have a wedding date set at this time, but I'd just like to prepare you. I am asking you to be my maiden of honor."

"Fantastic," replied Sheba, "it would be an honor to accept that position. Congratulations."

"Thank you," I replied. "Just imagine, Sheba, everyone will be calling me Mrs. Williams."

We both chuckled.

"Yeah, girl. No more single life. I want our wedding colors to be peach and grey," I told Sheba.

"So, how many people are going to be at the wedding?" asked Sheba.

"Oh, about one hundred fifty," I replied. "You know, Keno's family is really big."

"I know what you mean," stated Sheba. "Oh, Sabrina, I know that you are going to have the deejay at the reception play that song 'Whip Appeal.' You know, that song by Babyface that you and Keno always listen to."

"Girl, I am going to be on cloud nine on the wedding day. Between the cake, the pictures, the wedding party, and everything else that I'm going to be doing, I probably will not have time to remember to tell the DJ to play that song."

"Yeah, Sabrina, that day is going to be a very exciting day for the both of you."

"Okay, Sheba, I will call you later on. Goodnight."

I abruptly hung up the telephone. I prepared my bubble bath and relaxed. I played our song by Babyface, "Whip Appeal," as I sat in the warm bubble bath. "Whatever you want, it's alright with me, 'cause you got that whip appeal . . ."

The next morning, I woke up with a new outlook on life. I opened up my bedroom window. I could feel the cool breeze move across my face. I was special. I felt different. I finally felt like my life had been defined. The telephone rang. It was Keno. He was on his lunch hour. For some strange reason, the phone rang louder than usual.

"Hello," I stated as I answered the telephone.

"Hello, Sabrina," stated Keno, "I need to talk with you."

"About what?" I replied. I was so nervous about the way that he approached me, but I could not dare give him any clue that I was in any way concerned.

"You know, Sabrina, I love you so much that I am going to pick out a more expensive engagement ring for you, but before I do so, I need to sit down with you in person and go over a few things with you." Well, Keno for the most part was a very straight-forward young man with his words.

"Okay, Keno, I will call you when I finish my classes on tomorrow. Also, I am spending the night at my mother's home."

"Fine," replied Keno. All the while I was wondering, what could Keno want to talk to me about? Why would he want to replace the ring that he gave me? After all, Keno was all that I had, at least in my mind. I was desperate to find out what Keno wanted to talk to me about. I would do anything to keep him in my life.

It was a hot morning when Keno drove up to the school campus that I attended, in order to meet me for lunch. I had finished my classes for the day. When Keno arrived, I could smell the distinguished aroma of his cologne. His eyes appeared to have the same gleam that they had when we first met.

"Hello, Sabrina,"

"Hello, Keno," I replied with a subtle tremor in my voice, as I sat in the vehicle. This was the first time in my life that I actually felt like I was in love. I grew up in a single-parent home. My mother was alone, raising the two of us without my father, Mr. Barnes, as they called him. Mr. Barnes was a married man who had two children from a previous marriage. He also had a mistress who had a biological 19-year old son with him. She was also married. I always wondered why my mother had the two of us with a married man. Even though it was not correct in the eyes of God, I was glad to be part of the land of the living. Besides, my mother had been delivered from her past. Although he was not living with us, I still loved him. He was a "book smart" and a "street smart" man. I knew not to compare Keno with my father. Since meeting Keno, I had been spending less time with my father. I would usually speak with him at least once every two weeks. I vowed to wait until the wedding plans were made before "spilling the beans" about Keno and I being engaged. My father always appreciated the finished product, no matter what it was. During most of our conversations, I always kept dear old dad in the back of my mind.

The place where Keno and I were dining for lunch was what I considered sort of "shabby." "RIB SHACK" read the bold red letters on the front of the glass window. The withered menu taped to the splinter-surfaced wood door read "lunch special." I could not dare let Keno know how nervous I was about this meeting. My facial expression could not hide the way that I was feeling.

"Sabrina, let us get a table for two," exclaimed Keno.

"Fine," I replied.

"Waiter," shouted Keno, "we would like a booth, two for lunch." As the waiter escorted us to the booth by the window, I noticed the freshly picked flowers placed in the center of the table. As we sat at the table, it began to get very cloudy, and shortly it began to rain. "Pitter-patter, pitter-patter," I heard as the large raindrops hit the window pane. The rain drops seemed as though they were getting louder, and louder.

The waiter asked, "May I get you something to drink?"

"Yes," Keno replied, "I will have a glass of lemonade."

"I will have a glass of iced tea," I stated as I glanced at the large raindrops on the window pane. As the waiter walked away, I stared Keno in the eyes. For some strange reason, his pupils were much larger than usual.

"Sabrina, I have been thinking. You already know that I am working full time during the day, and going to school part-time in the evening. I respect the fact that you are in college full-time. You know, Sabrina, I am in need of a little help from you financially. You know, I just believe that we should be doing the same things. I think that you should get a full time job and transfer from Wagner College into a City University school. You could take your classes part-time until you obtain your degree. Just imagine, Sabrina, we could save some money and get our own apartment."

Well, I was so shocked. I could not believe what Keno was saying to me. I did not understand where this request came from. It seemed as if it came out of the raindrops that were continuously hitting the window pane. Why would Keno ask me to transfer from the private school that I was attending, especially since I was at the end of my junior year in college. Besides, I worked so hard to get into the school that I attend, and it is a private school. Many people would be very thankful to be in my shoes. Not to mention the scholarships, and the grants that I was given towards my tuition. Although I was very disturbed about his request, I pretended to be elated.

"Keno, that would be a great idea. Besides, we could plan our wedding in privacy, in our own apartment."

"Sabrina, I am so happy that you are in agreement with my vision concerning our future."

As Keno finished his sentence, the waiter replied, "What will you be ordering today?" Although all of a sudden I was in no mood to eat, I abruptly responded,

"I will have a cheeseburger and fries with a fruit punch, please."

Keno stated, "I will have the same." As the waiter picked up the menus and walked away, Keno looked into my eyes and said, "Sabrina, this is great!!" We sat in silence for about fifteen minutes. I could sense Keno's mind racing to and fro. Finally, Keno decided to break the silence.

"You know, Sabrina, I think that I would have a good chance of getting you a job with the agency that I work with. As a matter of fact, there is a clerical position downtown that is available. The starting salary is eighteen thousand dollars a year. If we add up the twenty-five thousand dollars a year that I make, we would have forty three thousand dollars a year in total. We would be able to get a nice apartment, save some money, and be independent," Keno stated as the waiter placed our meal in front of us. "I have a great rapport with upper-management within the agency that I work for. With your skills, and my reputation, you would have no problem getting hired, in no time. You know, Sabrina, I could even get you an interview, as soon as next week. The director of the department, Mr. Greenstein, is a very nice man. How's that sound?" Well, Keno was pretty charming with his words. I couldn't dare disappoint him by dismissing his proposal.

"Alright," I said, as I put a greasy French fry into my mouth.

Keno replied, "I will contact Mr. Greenstein on next week in order to schedule the interview."

"That sounds great." While Keno was driving me to my mother's house, I suddenly felt as if my entire world with Keno was slowly collapsing.

"Oh, Sabrina," Keno exclaimed as he glanced at my butter-creamed complexion face. "Don't forget to bring the rest of your clothes from your mom's house, next week when you come over since you will be moving permanently into my mother's home with me, until we get our new apartment." As Keno drove away, I could feel the sudden discomfort of my mind struggling with my emotions regarding the situation.

A week had quickly passed by. I was on my way to Keno's mother's house—permanently. It was a bright sunny day. As I approached the front door of Keno's mother's house, holding my suitcase, I noticed the numbers on the battered heavy wooden door which read, 455 South Avenue. The numbers on the house appeared much larger than usual for some strange reason. Before I was able to ring the bell, Ms. Williams abruptly opened the door. She obviously had been watching me approach the front gate, from the window upstairs.

"Hello, Sabrina."

"Hello, Ms. Williams."

"So," stated Ms. Williams, as she glanced at me from the side of her almond-shaped eye. "Keno tells me that you will be starting a full time job with the City. That is so nice. You know, consider yourself lucky that you pulled that one off so fast," she stated as she clapped her hands together. "So, is it true that you are going to transfer to a City School"? "You may lose some credits, and how many people from the Stapleton projects where you grew up actually get a chance to step foot into Wagner College?"

Well, Ms. Williams must have been reading my mind. Although I agreed with her regarding her notion, I would not dare tell her. I was determined to play along with their game, as long as I could get away with it.

"So," stated Ms. Williams. Once you start your new job, you and Keno could save some money, so that you can get an apartment together, and plan a life for yourselves. "How lovely," stated Ms. Williams as she glanced out of the front window, pretending to be preoccupied with something, or someone outside. Ms. Williams was really starting to irritate me with her phony best wishes. I never really felt as if Ms.

Williams genuinely appreciated my kindness, or presence. I always felt as if she always pretended that she liked me. I guess that we both just tolerated each other for Keno's sake.

"Well," I softly stated, "I have not confirmed a definite date with Keno, regarding transferring schools, or accepting a full-time position." Ms. Williams appeared to have no problem with jumping to conclusions.

"Well," stated Ms. Williams, "Keno is upstairs. By the way, Sabrina, I am going out with Rosa this weekend. I will need you to cook for John and Sandra; oh, and you know the routine, please make sure that their hair is combed." I could slowly feel the mark "SLAVE" being branded on my forehead, and "MOLLY MAID" branded on my chest. As I proceeded up the stairs, I could hear Keno speaking on the telephone.

"Yeah, Marky," Keno loudly shouted, "I think that it would be a great idea. Okay, we'll see you on tomorrow." As Keno was putting down the telephone, I entered the bedroom.

"Hey, what' up, Sabrina, how was your day?"

"My day was fine," I stated as Keno plopped a quick, wet kiss on my lips. Before I could even utter another word, Keno exclaimed,

"I was just speaking with my old buddy Marky. You know, the guy that you saw me with at the club back in the day," he said as he softly chuckled. "You might have heard me talking about him. He is also engaged. He and his fiancée will be in town for about two months. I thought that it would be a great idea if all four of us went out, in order to celebrate." Keno always had a way of dictating plans before confirming them with me. "Sabrina, we have arranged to meet on tomorrow evening, at the Placid Restaurant, across the street from the Underground Club in Manhattan." As Keno finished speaking, *I slowly* began to remember his old buddy Marky from the past. It was a gloomy Saturday, about four months ago, when I visited Keno. In my mind, I was really looking forward to spending the entire evening with him, alone. As I walked up to the front entrance and rang the bell, I could hear Keno's favorite "house music" playing very loudly. "Break for Love" was the song playing. Keno loved to dance, and I could feel his energy pierce through my chest from the front entrance. I hastily rang the bell again. Evidently, there was nobody home with Keno. He was obviously unable to hear the bell, because the music was too loud. I turned the doorknob, and to my surprise, the door was open. I proceeded to walk up the creaky-sounding steps into Keno's room. As I entered the room, I saw Keno dancing to his house music, as he was getting dressed. Well, I thought, it's only four o'clock in the afternoon. If I were one to go to clubs, it would be definitely too early for me to be partying.

"Keno, what's up with all of that loud music, and why are you all dressed up?" Keno had on a pair of neatly pressed black dress slacks, a silk, white turtle-neck shirt, and a multi-colored vest. My man was in style. He had on the latest floor-shine shoes that the average "pretty boy" would kill for. Keno sported the fade haircut, which was very popular among the young men of the eighties. The style really looked good on him.

"Sabrina, I know that I promised that we'd go to a movie on tonight, but Marky called me and I have portrayed tonight as "boys' night out.""

Well, I was up hauled. The least he could have done was called me at my mother's house in order to save me a trip over here, only to discover that my evening had been ruined. Who was I fooling? Any other time, I would stay home, and wait for Keno to return from his escapades. I was determined that on this night, no matter what, Sabrina would not stay home and wait for him.

"So, what time are you and Marky meeting?"

18

"Oh," Keno replied, "I'd say that I should be leaving here at about five o'clock so that I could pick him up from his Aunt Betty's house in Bayonne, New Jersey."

Well, Keno drove a 1988 two-door, light-blue Nissan Maxima. He was pretty good at maneuvering his faithful stick shift vehicle.

"So, Keno, where are you and Marky going to hang out at?" I asked with a phony smile.

"Oh, we're going to meet a couple of the fellas at the good old Underground Club in Manhattan. You know, just to chill out and catch up on the latest dance moves."

I trusted Keno, but I didn't trust myself. I was a quite attractive female, but Keno, he had a face that the females lived for. We would ride on the bus together at times, and I would literally catch other females giving him the complete stare-down.

"Yeah, I know what you mean," I said abruptly. "It's been a while since I spent time with my best friend, Sheba. I know what you mean."

Before I knew it, the grandfather clock struck five o'clock p.m. Keno was doing the finishing touches on his outfit.

"Well, Sabrina, I will see you when I get back."

Whenever Keno went out on "boys' night," I never saw him until the next morning. I was determined that it would not happen. No, not on this boys' night out. I would not sit up and wait for him to come home.

"Okay, Keno, have a nice time," I stated after he gave me a quick kiss on my gold colored painted lips. I hastily followed him downstairs and locked the door behind him. As I walked back up the stairs, I could hear Keno start the motor of his car. When I entered into the bedroom, I looked out of the window, into the dreary driveway. Keno was backing the vehicle out into the street. Finally, he was clear out of the driveway, on the way to his destination. I immediately ran back downstairs into the kitchen and picked up the telephone. I dialed my best friend Sheba's number as fast as I could. "Ring, ring," the phone rang at least five times. As I listened to the number of telephone rings increase, I could feel the sigh of desperation consuming my mind. I was hoping that Sheba was at home. Finally, the answering machine picked up. "Hi, I can't come to the phone, but please leave a message." I began leaving a message when Sheba abruptly intercepted the answering machine.

"Hello," exclaimed Sheba with a raspy Jamaican accent.

"Thank God," I shouted. "Sheba, this is Sabrina."

"Hey girl, what's up?" replied Sheba.

"I need your help," I demanded.

"What is it?"

"Keno and his friends are going out to the Underground Club, you know the reggae club over in Manhattan."

"Yeah, but since when does Keno like reggae?"

"He really doesn't but on Friday nights the club has a house music marathon, or something. Anyway, I wanted to know if you would come with me to the club so that I could spy on him. I mean, I trust him but I just want to make sure that he has no hidden agendas when it comes to other females. I don't know, but sometimes I feel like there is somebody else. I guess it's just the club 'thing' that I'm uncomfortable with."

Well, Sheba was a hard-core Jamaican yardee. She was born in Jamaica, West Indies, but she came to this country when she was about eight years old. She left the island of Jamaica, but the island never left her. Sheba loved reggae music. She would not dare refuse to accompany me to the reggae club. I have known Sheba for at least ten years. She practically grew up with me in the Stapleton Projects. I knew most of her family who lived in the States at the time and she knew my family, including my father, Mr. Barnes. Basically, I trusted her.

"You want to spy, Sabrina?" questioned Sheba with an undertone of motherly love.

"Yeah, spy," I abruptly responded. "I do not think that it is too bad of an idea. I mean—what is the worst thing that could happen? I could bust him on a date with a female that I probably know." I could feel my imagination running wildly, into information that was not even valid until Sheba abruptly interrupted me.

"Sabrina, I will go with you to the club; however, don't blame me if you catch him out on a date with one of our male math teachers from junior high school." We both chuckled. "Thanks, Sheba, you're the greatest. I am going down to the car rental shop. I will call you once I get the vehicle in my possession. I already know the directions to the club. I mean it's not that far, after all. Sheba, start getting dressed for the occasion, and be certain that you are dressed to impress."

"Okay," Sheba excitedly responded. "I will wait for your call."

As I hung up the telephone, I could feel a big chill of revenge run up my spine. I planned to be the best dressed female in the club on tonight. I was convinced that there would be nobody else to compete with me for my man. I abruptly ran upstairs and opened the closet door. I picked across two dresses, one blue, one black. Nah, I was feeling in the mood to wear red. I quickly pushed back the two hangers and BAM, there it was—my beautiful red dress. My father bought this dress for me about one year ago. It was a red velvet dress that I picked out on the last time that he took me shopping. The dress had short sleeves and two sexy slits on each side. I picked up my black patent leather shoes from the bottom of the closet. I had already showered. I slipped on the sleek, red velvet dress, as I proudly looked into the full-length mirror. WOW. This dress really showed off my curves. I was surprised that I could still fit the dress. As a matter of fact, the dress fit me better than ever. I calmly put on my shoes, fixed my hair in a nice French roll, and added the finishing touches to my make-up.

I picked up the telephone and called the cab to take me to the car rental agency. I was dressed to kill. As I entered the car rental agency, I noticed a tall, thin white man with white hair standing at the back of the counter. He appeared weary from a long, hard day of car rental customer service. "BOB," read the name tag pinned to his white dress shirt.

"Hello," I stated as I walked up to the front desk. "I would like to rent a car for the weekend."

"Well, young lady," he cheerfully responded, "we only have one car left. As a matter of fact, consider yourself lucky. Someone just canceled reservations just one hour ago. We have a red 1989 Maxima, fully loaded."

WOW . . . I was so preoccupied with spying on Keno that I did not even think about making reservations.

"Well, sir, how much would it cost to rent the vehicle for the weekend?" I asked with a subtle grin.

"Two hundred fifty dollars," he replied as he gestured a crooked smile. "You will need a valid credit card, along with a valid driver's license."

Valid credit cards were no problem for me. After all, I had every credit card that you could think of with limits exceeding $3,500.00 each. Pretty good for a college student. It seemed like all of us college students at Wagner College had no problem getting credit cards.

"No problem," I replied as I handed him my Visa card, and driver's license. It seemed like the process of renting a car was taking so long, although I was only at the rental agency for about fifteen minutes. Finally, after thirty minutes of him verifying all of my information, Bob approached me waiting at the counter.

"It all checks out good," he stated as he handed me back my driver's license and credit card. "I'll drive around, and you'll be set to take the vehicle."

As I walked outside, around to the back of the building, Bob drove up in the glossy, red Maxima. It was even more beautiful than I had imagined, almost matching the exact color of my red velvet dress.

"Well," stated Bob as he hopped out of the car, "she's all yours. All of your paperwork is here—I just need your signature. The car is due back by 12 noon on Sunday."

"Thank you," I replied as I quickly signed my name on the receipts.

"Have a good time," shouted Bob as I drove the car out of the lot.

The vehicle was so beautiful. As I sat in the vehicle, I changed the radio station to many different stations. After about five minutes of trying to find the best music to listen to, I finally found a song that was appealing to my ears. One hour had already passed by since I had spoken to Sheba. After all of the time that I spent renting the car, Sheba should have been dressed and ready to go. I drove down the spiral road, and spotted a payphone. I abruptly got out of the vehicle and dialed Sheba's telephone number.

"Hello."

"Hi, this is Sabrina, I picked up the rental, and I am on my way to pick you up from home."

"I should be ready in five minutes," stated Sheba in a loud tone of voice. "Sabrina, when you get in front of my house, just beep the horn, and I will come right downstairs."

"Okay," I replied.

"I will see you soon."

"Alright," I stated. I anxiously entered into the vehicle. I thought to myself, wow, this is going to be a great night. I could not wait to get to the Underground Club. As I slowly drove up to Sheba's house, I noticed her standing outside. Sheba was dressed like she just walked out of the fashion plate magazine. She was attractive and always looked nice in her clothes. Although Sheba lived in an upper-middle class neighborhood, there were still some people who lived there who I declared as "ghetto."

"Ooh girl, where are you going?" asked one of Sheba's nosy neighbors as she held the beer can up to her pale-brown face.

"I'm going out, somewhere you can't go," Sheba angrily stated as she got into the vehicle.

"Some things never change," I stated in an abrupt voice. "You can take some people out of the ghetto, but you can't take the ghetto out of some people." We both laughed.

"Hey, Sabrina, nice wheels you got here. We're riding in style."

"Yes, we certainly are. I was quite lucky. Someone canceled at the last minute, and here we are riding instead of taking the ferry, and train."

Sheba and I were enjoying the scenery as we crossed the Verrazano Bridge. There was very little traffic on the highway. We were having a great time enjoying the music, and talking about the good old school days. Before I knew it, we were approaching the club. "UNDERGROUND" read the gold-glittered sign on the flat-top building.

"There goes the Club," shouted Sheba, as we parked the vehicle in front of the parking meter.

I began to feel afraid. Many questions began to run across my mind. What if I caught Keno in an act that he could not explain? What if he were upset that I even came to the club? How would I react if I saw something that I did not want to see? It was too late to turn back. I was already here. Sheba and I attempted to walk up to the front door of the

Underground Club. We could hear the loud sound of the reggae music playing as we walked towards the back of the long line of about fifty people. Finally, the line got shorter after a twenty minute wait.

As Sheba and I approached the entrance, the bouncer asked, "ID, please, and the admission is ten dollars each." He was a short, stocky, fair-skinned young man about in his late twenties. He spoke with a slight lisp. I handed him my ID, and Sheba did the same. The bouncer shouted, "You two ladies can go in for free. Have a nice time tonight."

As we approached the entrance of the club I noticed the blue neon lights which illuminated the entire dance floor. The crowd was so dense, and we had to literally push our way over to the bar. I was so excited. The sound of the music slowly began to crowd my mind. I felt the beat of the music penetrate my soul. As we walked towards the bar, I heard a man order a drink.

"Vodka on the rocks, please." Ha, ha, ha shouted the two men that sat near by.

As Sheba and I walked up to the bar, the bartender grudgingly asked, "What will you two ladies be drinking tonight?"

I responded, "I'll have an amaretto on the rocks." That was my favorite social drink.

"I'll have the same," replied Sheba. The room was dimly lit and the people who were sitting around the bar appeared to be too comfortable. They almost appeared to be permanent residents. They were probably sitting there all day. Sheba and I decided to get up from the bar with our drinks and walk around. As we were walking around the club, I looked to my left and noticed a young man and young lady dancing. He appeared to have her pinned to the wall. It almost seemed as if they were having sexual intercourse. As we walked further into the crowd, we could see many people intensely dancing to the beat of the music. They acted as if they were contestants in a dance contest, and they all had to win. As we approached the ramp, we entered into another area of the club.

Sheba shouted, "Hey, Sabrina, there's Keno." As she finished her statement I could feel my body run bitter-cold, as if a numbness took hold of me.

"Yeah, you're right. That is Keno." As I looked in the direction where Keno was, I noticed him standing there with two young men, and a female who appeared to have had trouble with keeping her hands away from Keno's face. I kept wondering if I should scream now, or wait until later. I figured that I would wait until later. Keno was going home with me tonight. As Sheba and I approached Keno and his boys, he glanced at me as if he had seen a ghost.

"Hello, Keno," I exclaimed. Sheba stood there next to me, speechless. Well, Keno was just too through with me. He looked at me as if he wanted to disappear. Before Keno could respond, the female who was standing with Keno and his friends abruptly slurred.

"Hey, Keno, who is she? When are we going to get up out of this place?" She was dressed in spiked-high heels, and wore half of a dress. She must have bought it at a half-price sale, I thought. She obviously had too much to drink. Before I could get a chance to verbally attack her, Keno shouted, "Yo, my girl is here. I will check you out some other time." I had to really ask myself what would have happened if I did not show up at the club. I started to wonder if Keno would have cheated on me that night if I never showed up. A large part of me, deep down inside of me gave him the benefit of the doubt, and denied the truth—even when it stared me in the face. If I didn't catch him in the act, I never accused him. I was in denial. As she abruptly walked away, she blew Keno a kiss.

"So, Sabrina, what made you come here tonight? What did you expect to see? Did you find what you were looking for?"

The sound of the music became intensely louder. Although I was very upset, I could not show it. I felt as if I had to pretend that seeing him with someone else did not bother me.

"I just thought that I would surprise you, by meeting you here. I even rented a car. I hope that you are not upset, Keno." I always had a way of hoping, when it came to Keno. I was slowly beginning to realize that my insecurities from someplace deep in my subconscious were beginning to surface.

"Sabrina, I'm not upset at you. I'm just surprised to see you here, that's all." Keno appeared to be experiencing a slight anxiety attack, when all of a sudden he abruptly stated, "Sabrina, let me introduce you to my long-time friend Marky. Marky, this is my girl, Sabrina. Sabrina, this is Marky."

"Nice meeting you," I softly stated.

Marky was a short, stocky young man. He sported a low-faded haircut. He held a drink in each hand, and spoke very loudly. "So, I have heard a lot about you, Sabrina, when is the wedding date?"

"Oh, I'm not really sure," I grudgingly replied. "Keno and I are in the process of discussing our future. Trust me, as soon as we set a date, you will be one of the first people to know."

"Oh, I just love Southern Comfort whiskey," shouted Marky as he walked towards the exit door of the club. I could literally smell the liquor seeping through the pores of his sweaty body. "Yeah, Sabrina, Marky is known for sweatin' the Southern Comfort." We all laughed.

"Well, we all need to be headed for home," said Keno. I glanced at my watch. The time read 1:30 a.m. I was tired. I just wanted to go home and relax with Keno. Sheba drove the vehicle, while Keno and I sat in the back seat. Marky had hitched a ride with one of his cousins who was surprisingly sober. It seemed to be a long ride home, back to Staten Island. Everyone in the car was quiet. There was no music playing, no laughing, or talking. As we drove along the highways, Keno stared out of the window. I, on the other hand, was staring out of the window closest to me. I felt a calm, and peaceful feeling as I glanced at the cars passing by. As we drove along the Verrazano Bridge, although it was dark, I noticed the tranquility of the water. The waves rippled peacefully. Before I knew it, Sheba was paying the toll in order to cross the bridge to Staten Island. After about twenty minutes, Sheba was finally driving up to Keno's house. I decided to stay over Keno's place, since it was so late. We were back in familiar territory. I was more than relieved.

"Thank you for driving back to Staten Island, Sheba."

"No problem, Sabrina," Sheba replied in her famous Jamaican country accent.

"You can keep the car until tomorrow. Just call me and we can both take it back on tomorrow." I was just too tired and disgusted to prolong the conversation. I began slurring my speech.

"Good night," Keno exclaimed, "good night."

We both walked up to the front entrance of the house. Keno took out his bunch of keys, and opened the door. We proceeded to walk up the stairs, with Keno leading the way. As we entered the front of the bedroom door, Keno pushed me into the door and onto the king-sized bed. We kissed, and he ran his hand down the side of my thigh. Before I knew it, we were making passionate love together. Wow, I thought, his expression towards me was worth more than words. Keno did not need to say "I love you." Why? Because I already knew. Keno and I fell fast asleep.

I was not too thrilled about Keno and I meeting up with Marky and his fiancée. Since Keno seemed so excited about us hanging out with Marky and his future wife, I made it my business to cooperate. It was a cool Friday evening when Keno and I met Marky and his fiancée at the famous Placid Restaurant. As Keno and I walked towards the restaurant, I could see Marky waving, attempting to get Keno's attention. Finally, Keno and Marky caught each other's attention.

"Well, hello," stated Marky as Keno and I approached the front entrance of the restaurant.

"Nice meeting you again," I replied.

"My fiancée is sitting over there waiting for us at the table." We all quickly walked over to the table where Marky's fiancée was seated. She appeared to be a slim-built female, with big brown eyes. Her complexion was light brown. Her eyes resembled two almonds. Her makeup looked too perfect for the occasion. I started to feel like one of her competitors in a what would be fashion show. She was dressed in a white laced blouse. What was I worried about? After all, I was only here to please my man, Keno. I just wanted the evening to quickly pass by. We were all seated at a round table. I could smell the aroma of the freshly picked flowers that were placed in the middle of the table. The glare of the candles that were on the table gave each of our faces a glow of mystery.

"So," exclaimed Marky, "this is my fiancée, Stephanie. Stephanie, this is my good friend, Keno, and his fiancée Sabrina."

"Hi, Sabrina, it's a pleasure to meet you," replied Stephanie in a country-southern accent. "I have heard so much about you, Sabrina, and I think that it is so sweet that you would just drop out of college and get a full time job, just to please your man. You're a good girl, because if I were in the private school that you are in—Wagner College—you know how many people would love to be in your shoes? The cost for one credit could buy me a condo."

Everyone chuckled, except me. All of a sudden, I felt the urge to get up and leave the restaurant. Instead, I kept my cool, and remained seated. I was very upset. Keno and I never came to a conclusion regarding my leaving college. Besides, she had the story all mixed up. I decided to have some fun, and play along with Keno's game. At least for the evening.

"Yeah, Stephanie," I replied, "I am not actually leaving college, but I will be transferring to a City college, so that I may work full time during the day, and go to school part-time during the evening."

"Yes," replied Keno, "Sabrina is doing a great thing. We would be able to save some money together so that we could get an apartment. I am looking forward to spending the future with Sabrina."

"That's cool," stated Marky as the waiter approached our table.

"So, what can I get you all to drink?"

"We will have a pitcher of cola, if you don't, mind," said Keno. We all agreed to order a variety of Buffalo wings. After all, I was in no mood to eat. I really just wanted to get home, in order to confront Keno concerning my transferring from Wagner College. There was silence during most of the time that we were eating dinner. I had made up my mind that I would not have much of anything to say, until I got home. As we were finishing our meal, the waiter brought the check.

"Is there anything else I can bring out for you all?"

"No, that would be all," exclaimed Keno as he took his credit card out of his wallet. "It's on me." We all got up from the table, and walked towards the exit.

"Keno," stated Marky, "thanks for coming out to have a bite to eat with us. I really appreciate you and Sabrina's company."

"Take care," shouted Stephanie as we walked out of the restaurant. We walked out into the parking lot, and got into Keno's vehicle.

"Keno, we need to talk about a few issues concerning my leaving Wagner College."

"I know, Sabrina, as soon as we get home, I would like us to have a nice long talk."

We arrived at home within a half hour. We both changed our clothes into matching sweat suits that we bought from The Big Apple Bazaar.

"Sabrina, I just want to let you know that I really love you, and I'm looking forward to us being together for the rest of our lives," stated Keno as he embraced me closely.

"Keno," I replied, as I abruptly moved away from him, "we need to be on the same page regarding our future. First, you tell your mother that I'm leaving school, without even discussing the issue with me. Today, while we were out with Marky and Stephanie, I had to listen to her go on, and on about how she heard that I was leaving school. Keno, why didn't you discuss this issue with me before you told everyone that I was leaving school, in order to get a full time job?" Keno looked at me as if he were surprised that I actually was questioning him.

"Sabrina, I did not intend on offending you at all. If I did, I apologize. I just wanted to be positive by claiming the desire that I have for you to cooperate with the plans that I made for our future." That was the problem. Keno was making the plans for our future alone. I came too far into this relationship, in order to disagree with Keno.

"Well, Sabrina, you wouldn't believe. Do you remember the Director of Personnel from the agency that I work for?"

"No, not really," I replied.

"Mr. Greenstein, the one with all of the power. I told him all about you. "You know, how smart you are, and that you need to gain a full time position within the agency, and that we were engaged to become married. He was really receptive.

You know what, Sabrina; he even scheduled an interview for you on next Thursday, at 1:00 p.m."

I started to feel trapped—like a little girl left home all alone, sitting in a playpen. I did not have the strength to tell Keno that I would not accept his offer to go to the interview. I felt obligated to cooperate, even though I did not want to. I was eager to finish the conversation. I perceived that I had to remain calm and agree to his protocol, not realizing or caring how dangerous this situation could become.

"Okay, Keno, that sounds really exciting. Give me the information so that I can prepare myself."

About one week had passed, and it was the day before the interview was scheduled. Although I was not too thrilled about going to the interview, I found enough courage to convince myself that this was the correct path to follow. I had forced myself to become so excited about the situation. I decided to visit my mother in order to share the good news. It was a cold, dark, gloomy evening when I went to visit my mother. As I rode up the elevator to the seventh floor, I began to feel a slight sense of urgency to appear into my mother's presence. As the elevator ascended to the seventh floor, I became anxious. I stepped out of the elevator, and knocked on the door, "7C." My mother had the usual shrewd look on her face.

"Hi, Sabrina," exclaimed my mother. She appeared to be quite content on this cloudy evening. It was evident that the good news that I was going to give her concerning my decision to get a full time job would make her even more proud of me.

"Come in, sit down, don't act like a stranger." I sat down in my usual chair, the suede, yellow rocking chair that my sister and I fought over for many of our childhood years. The chair had a permanent impression of both of our gerri-curl hair activated- gel hairstyles from the early 1980's. It was evident that we had spent a lot of time sitting in the yellow rocking chair.

My mother was always receptive to listening to my problems. I had a lot of respect for her and always took her advice as needed. I was hoping that my mother would tell me what my ears wanted to hear.

Either way, I would take her advice regarding my situation. I always respected my mother's opinion.

"Hello, Sabrina," said my mother with a calm look on her pre-senior aged face.

"Hey mom, what's up?" I replied. I always wanted my mother to believe that everything in my life was going perfect, even if it wasn't. For some strange reason, I was always able to hide the truth regarding what was really always going on in my drama-filled life. I believe that my mother always knew what was really going on, but never exposed it. She was a woman that I always looked up to. She was the true PROVERBS woman that the Bible book of Proverbs literally bragged about.

"Mom, I just wanted to let you know that Keno landed me a really great job. He knows this 'big wig' that oversees a department within the organization that he works for. *Can you believe it?*" I exclaimed in a loud voice. "He was actually able to land me a job interview . I plan on transferring to a CUNY college. I could go to school part-time during the evening. I could work full-time during the day. Just think of it, Keno and I could move into our own apartment together, and plan for our future." Based on my performance in the presence of my mother, I convinced myself into believing that I was making the right decision regarding my plans to be with Keno in the future. The expression that was on my mother's face was worth more than words. She appeared to have lost her best friend in an unfortunate battle.

"Sabrina," my mother softly stated. "I understand that you really love Keno, but let me be honest with you." My mother's voice became louder and stronger. "You have one year left before you graduate from college. Sabrina, do you remember how excited you were when you first got accepted to Wagner College? Do you remember how many of your classmates that you grew up with here, in the Stapleton Projects got the opportunity like you did, to get into a school like that?"

I began to remember that nobody in my class actually received the opportunity that I had. I began to wonder if I was actually crazy for even considering to go along with Keno's plan.

"If Keno really loved you, he would wait until you graduate. You only have one year before you graduate. Sabrina, I love you, and you know this. I really want the best for you. Let me say this also. If you leave that school, and go along with Keno's plan, you will be the sorriest black woman that ever walked this earth."

As usual, I always respected whatever my mother told me whenever she gave me advice. There was something different about the tone of her voice *this time*. I clearly heard the sense of urgency in her voice. I had no choice but to take her advice. I was still going to play Keno's game by going to the job interview that he had already set up, just for his sake.

"Mom, I sincerely would like to thank you so much for your advice."

"You are very welcome, Sabrina. I just really hope that you take my advice to heart."

"I will, mom," I stated as I kissed her on her rosy colored high-boned cheek and got up in order to walk towards the double-lock bolted front door.

"Well, mom, I will speak to you soon, again thanks, and I love you." Well, that was easy enough, I thought, well at least on the surface. At this point, I was starting to feel confused. I was confused about everything. Would I be making the right choice by even going to the interview? If I didn't go to the interview, how would that make Keno feel? Did I really want to go to the interview at all? These were some of the many questions that began to surface.

As I approached the house where Keno and I resided, along with his family, I began to feel sick to my stomach. I walked up the steps, and unlocked the weather-beaten front door. Before I could enter the door, I noticed Keno, standing there with three helium-filled balloons. "Congratulations" read the bold letters on the balloons. I was so startled, I did not say a word.

"Hey, Sabrina, many congratulations to you on your new job. I know that you did not go to the interview yet, but I know that you are going to ace that interview. That's a given. I know that Mr. Greenstein is going to hire you."

"Thanks for the encouragement, Keno," I stated as I blew him a kiss.

"So, Sabrina, are you nervous about the interview"?

"No way," I stated in a low, but coy voice. "I still have some time to prepare myself. It's Wednesday, and tomorrow is the interview," I nervously replied. "You know something, Sabrina, this interview means a lot to me. It's actually going to determine our future together. As I mentioned before, we will be able to save money, so that we could move in together, and prepare for our future. I have even prepared myself to purchase you a more expensive ring."

It suddenly occurred to me that Keno and I were on different pages of life. We were speaking different languages. Even though I noticed the differences in our mind-sets, I was not prepared to let him go, or disappoint him. I decided to play his game, as long as I could last.

It was a beautiful Thursday morning, the day of my interview. The weather was warm, and the sun was shining brightly. When I opened the window, I could feel the warm breeze brush across my face. The aroma of the freshly-cut grass filled my nostrils. Keno was getting ready for work, and I had decided not to go to any classes on that particular day. I just wanted to get the interview over, and done with. It was about nine o'clock in the morning. Keno was obviously running late for work.

"Okay, Sabrina," stated Keno as he rushed down the stairs, "good luck at the interview. Call me at the office when you're finished. The address and directions to the interview are right there on the table."

"Okay," I replied, in a mono-toned voice. I began to feel nervous about the whole situation. I decided to take my shower, and prepare myself for the interview. Finally, I was dressed. I wore a white business-style shirt, with a navy blue knee-length skirt. My shoes were just right for the occasion. They were a pair of casual black penny-loafers. As soon as I was dressed, I called a cab to the Staten Island Ferry. The boat ride was very relaxing. "Lady Liberty" appeared to be even more glamorous standing under the grey clouds in the middle of the harbor. Although I was enjoying the boat ride, it seemed as if the ride was a little longer than usual. As we approached the harbor in Manhattan, the boat made its faithful, loud bump into the logs on the pier. Everyone walked off of the ferry as if they had someplace important to go, except for me. I strolled off of the boat as if I had all day to reach my destination. After all, it was only 11:30 in the morning. I arrived at the #1 train station, and waited on the platform with about fifty other straphangers. After about four stops on the train, I finally reached my destination.

"Next stop, Franklin Street," stated the train conductor in a loud, raspy voice.

I got up, and walked up onto the street level. The address that I was looking for was 455 Franklin Street. I walked down the crowded, busy street, and on the left side of the street was the building. I decided to "kill some time" by going over to the diner on the corner for a cup of coffee and a doughnut. Finally it was 12:30. I abruptly walked out of the diner, over to 455 Franklin Street. As I approached the skyscraper-styled building, the security guard stared at me, as if I were an unexpected visitor. I proceeded to walk over to the elevators, when he stopped me.

He was a tall, white man who appeared to have had no sleep within the past two days.

"Excuse me, miss, do you have an appointment to see someone in the building?"

"Yes, I'm scheduled to interview with Mr. Greenstein," I stated as I reached into my tote bag and pulled out a crumpled piece of paper, containing the information regarding the interview.

"What floor is he on?" asked the guard.

"He's on the fifth floor; I believe he's with the Parking Violations Bureau," I stated.

"Oh, yes, you're absolutely correct," the man stated as he browsed through a black and white marble notebook. "I will just need to see a piece of identification."

I showed the man my driver's license.

"You can go up to the fifth floor, over there," he stated as he pointed to a pair of elevators. "Good luck on your interview," he yelled as he turned away from me.

The rickety elevator doors opened and I pressed #5. The door opened, and I noticed a bright sign which read; PARKING VIOLATIONS BUREAU. I got off of the elevator, and walked towards a woman who was seated at a desk. She was a dark-skinned woman who was dressed in what appeared to be business-casual attire. I assumed that she was Mr. Greenstein's secretary.

"Hi, may I help you?" she politely asked.

"Yes, I am here for an interview. I believe it's for the data entry position."

"What is your name?" she demanded.

"Sabrina. Sabrina Matheson."

"Oh, yes," she stated as she looked over a long white sheet of paper containing about fifty names. "Just sit right here," she stated as she pointed to the set of chairs that were positioned directly across from her. "Mr. Greenstein will be right with you."

I began to feel nervous. After waiting for about ten minutes, my palms began to sweat. Finally, Mr. Greenstein appeared. He was a heavy set white man, who appeared to be in his mid-fifties. He wore a black yarmulke on the crown of his head. The hair on the sides of his head was white. His moustache and beard were a perfect match. His white shirt appeared to have been abused by the sweat, caused by the previous summers.

"Hi, Sabrina," he stated as if he had known me for years. "I'm glad to see that you showed up for the interview early. That's a plus in my book. Just for the record, Keno already sent me your resume. I was very impressed with your work history, and present educational background. I just wanted to place the face with the resume," he cunningly stated. "The job is yours," he cheerfully shouted. "Would you be able to start on Monday?"

I suddenly began to feel as if Keno had set me up. This was no interview. This was just an arrangement that Keno had made behind my back for selfish reasons. I had made up my mind that I was not going to take the job. I would not tell Mr. Greenstein, but I would tell Keno when I got back to the house.

"I would be able to start on next Thursday, Mr. Greenstein," I stated as I glared at the brightly colored still-life painting that was hanging on the withered wall.

"That would be great, Sabrina. When you come in on next Thursday, please be here at 8:30 a.m. You will also need to bring your original birth certificate, and Social Security card. If you have a driver's license, it would be a good idea if you also bring it."

"Okay, Mr. Greenstein, I will see you on next week. Thank you for your time."

"I will see you soon, Sabrina."

It was a long ride back home on the train and the ferry. It seemed as if the people had nothing else better to do than to overcrowd the train's platform. I was mentally preparing myself for my telling Keno that I would not take the position that Mr. Greenstein offered me. I kept hearing my mother's voice saying, "If you transfer from Wagner College to a City school, you will be the sorriest black woman that ever walked this earth. If Keno really cared about you, he would wait." It seemed as if the closer that I got back to the house, the louder her voice became. Finally, I reached back to our place. When I entered into the house, Keno was sitting in the living room. He had a look on his face that I could not describe.

"Hey, Sabrina, how's it going? How did the interview go?" he asked, in a tone as if he had known all along that I had landed the position.

"Keno, there are some things that I need to discuss with you regarding this whole situation."

"What is it, Sabrina?" Keno abruptly exclaimed as he crossed his muscular arms.

"I really don't think that I should take the job. As a matter of fact, I'm not going to accept the position. I mean, Keno, if you really cared about me, you would wait for me. I'm a junior, for God's sake. Next year, I am going to graduate. You know that graduating from this school is very important to me. Also, if I transfer, I will lose credits."

"Sabrina, what the hell are you in a rush to graduate for?" Keno shouted in a harsh, angry monotone voice. "Sabrina, you act as if you are in a race to get out of college in four years. Nobody's in a race around here."

"I'm sorry, Keno, I just can't do it. My mother even agrees that if I did take the position, and work full time, I'd be making the wrong choice."

"What the hell does your mother have to do with this?" Keno frantically exclaimed. "She's not the one supporting you. I am. And you know something, Sabrina, it's getting a little bit too expensive. As a matter of fact, I don't want to do this anymore. You made me believe that you were in my corner. You made me go out of my way to convince Mr. Greenstein that you were perfect for the position that he interviewed you for. The engagement is off."

As I attempted to grab Keno by the arm, he quickly ran out of the house and slammed the door.

Three hours passed since I had seen Keno at the house. It was about eight o'clock in the evening when I finally fell asleep. I got up on the next morning, and got dressed for class. Keno was still not at home. I decided to pretend like we never had a disagreement. I spent the day just as I always did. I focused on my classes, enjoyed conversation with my classmates, and spent some time in the library. I was feeling like I really wanted to see Keno. In fact, I could not wait until I got home so that we could make up, and start all over again. Even though he said that the engagement was off, I still had hope. For some strange reason, I did not believe him.

I had finished my research at the library early. As I got off the bus, on the way to Keno's house where we resided together, I began to feel a sense of sadness. As I approached the house, I noticed a pile of clothes in the front of the house from a distance. As I got closer to the pile of clothing, I began to realize that the clothes belonged to me. Keno had literally dumped all of my clothes outside. I took out my keys in order to open the door, and surprisingly, my keys would not open the door. Keno had changed the locks. I began to feel a huge anxiety attack come upon me. I knocked on the neighbor's door, and asked to use the phone. I picked up the telephone anticipating that I would speak with Keno. The phone rang many times, and nobody answered. I called Sheba. Thank God that she was home.

"Sheba," I exclaimed in the middle of my sobbing, "it's a long story, and I can't even think right now. Keno broke off the engagement because I wouldn't take the job, and transfer schools. My clothes are all outside in the front of the house." I am at Ms. Yona's house next door.

"I'll be right over," Sheba screamed in a frantic voice, and slammed down the phone.

I was sobbing uncontrollably. "He threw my clothes outside, like I'm a dog, he didn't love me, there must be somebody else."

"Oh, my goodness," shouted the neighbor. Is there something that I can do for you, Sabrina? This is so terrible. "It will be okay," stated Ms. Yona.

Ms. Yona was an oriental woman who appeared to be in her mid-fifties. She's a neighbor who always said "good morning" when the morning wasn't going so good. She seemed like a nice person who was always polite. This was one day that I really appreciated Ms. Yona's kindness. She made me a cup of tea, and allowed me to wait in her home until Sheba would arrive. I was slowly beginning to finally realize that my world with Keno had collapsed right before my eyes. The anxiety that I was beginning to perceive regarding the situation was beginning to overwhelm me. I began to feel like I had lost my only connection to true life, and true love. It seemed as if Sheba was taking a long time to get to Ms. Yona's house. I didn't have any words for conversation. I just sat quietly, and waited for Sheba.

I sat by the large storm window in the living room. Ms. Yona's living room reminded me of a museum. She had very colorful paintings that appeared to be very expensive hanging on the walls. There were many glass items neatly placed in the wall unit. The tiles were made of heavy ceramic. I was constantly glancing into the front yard in great expectation of Sheba's arrival. It was as if I were a child, desperately waiting for my mother to pick me up from aftercare.

After about an hour, I noticed Sheba walk up to Ms. Yona's front door. She did not have on her best Sunday attire, but I was still glad to see her. She came to my rescue. I abruptly ran outside into the front yard in order to meet her.

"Sheba," I stated as I began to sob, "the wedding is off. Keno wants nothing to do with me. Look over there," I yelled as I pointed to the pile of clothes that were in the front yard next door. "Those are all of my clothes. He basically threw me out. I can't even get into the house," I screamed as I hastily threw the engagement ring into the bushes nearby.

"Where did all of this confusion come from?" Sheba hastily questioned.

As I attempted to explain myself, I noticed Keno drive up into the driveway, with his mother Ms. Williams in the front seat. She glanced at me and quickly turned away. As Keno got out of the vehicle, Sheba attempted to get his attention.

"Keno, may I speak with you?" Sheba politely asked.

"Right now, I don't have the time," he abruptly stated as he entered into the house.

As Ms. Williams was getting out of Keno's vehicle, she put on her sunglasses. She appeared to have had something very important to say, but was obviously having a difficult time in doing so. Finally, she got up enough nerve and spoke.

"Sabrina, I'm very sorry about what has happened. You can stay here until you get yourself together."

"Just like that?" I questioned in a desperate tone of voice. "Can't you talk to him? He won't even speak to me," I stated in a tremored voice.

"You know, Sabrina, Keno wants other things out of life. That's all I can say," she stated in a tone of voice which indicated that I had been set up all along.

As a result of the stress that I was experiencing, I could feel the blood in my veins starting to boil. It seemed as if Ms. Williams finally got the revenge that she had always wanted. Keno and I were history. Sheba and I began to swiftly pick up my clothes, and bring them into the front room of the house. After all of the clothes were piled up in the front room, Sheba and I sat in the living room.

"Sabrina, I just want you to know that this is not going to be easy for you. I want you to know that I'm here for you."

Even though I found her words to be quite soothing, I was too upset to even reply.

"Now you have to focus on moving forward. I'm not really clear on what happened here, but it's not making any sense to me." As Sheba finished her sentence, Keno walked down the stairs, and out of the house. I felt the immediate urge to get up, and run after him, but I didn't. Ms. Williams entered into the room where we were seated, and joined our conversation.

"Sabrina," stated Ms. Williams, "you can stay here, as I told you, until you get everything in order. As far as Keno, I already told you, he wants other things."

I was starting to believe that Ms. Williams was hiding something. She wanted me present for her convenience, but offered no sympathy for what I was experiencing.

"I'll just sit here for awhile, and then I will go back to my mother's house."

"Okay," replied Ms. Williams, "whatever you say," she stated in a monotone voice. "Sabrina, you are always welcome in my home. You can always visit whenever you like."

I was starting to believe that Ms. Williams was actually crazy.

"Well, I will be going," she yelled as she approached the front door in order to leave. "Before you go, just slam the door, and it will lock."

Sheba and I sat on the couch, in silence. Finally, the silence was broken.

"Sabrina, I am so sorry that this has happened to you."

"I know, Sheba, things happen in life, you know." I was trying to be strong but deep down inside, I felt as if I were breaking apart.

"If you like, Sabrina, I will bring your clothes to your mother's house."

"Thanks, just tell my mother that you're dropping off my clothes. You don't have to get into any details. I will explain everything to her when I get home."

Sheba hastily finished packing the clothes, and walked out of the front door. I wasn't sure if she had slam-locked the door. Basically I didn't care. When I heard the engine of her vehicle fade away, I walked into the kitchen, and sat by the window. I began to recall the great times that Keno and I had. I began to regret even turning down the position that Mr. Greenstein offered me. I began to regret ever even meeting Keno. I began to regret everything. I began to regret ever being born. The pain that I was experiencing was too much to bear. I figured that I'd end it. I noticed a butcher knife on the counter. As I looked over on the refrigerator, I noticed a telephone number. It was Marky's number. I grabbed the knife and began to run it across my left wrist. I figured for some strange reason that before I ended my life, I would call Marky and tell him what had happened between Keno and I. I have never called him in the past. I hardly knew him. I figured that it would be beneficial. My hands were shaking as I picked up the phone, in order to dial Marky's number. The phone rang, and finally someone answered. It was Marky.

"Hello, this is Marky."

"Hello, Marky, this is Sabrina, Keno's friend."

"Hi, Sabrina, how's everything?" he asked in a tone as if he had already known about our break-up.

"I just want you to know that Keno and I broke up, and I'm not taking it too well. I thought that I would be able to handle the pressure, but I'm having a really hard time dealing with this situation. I know that I only met you twice, but you are his friend. I need to talk to somebody about it."

"Sabrina, you have to move on. Don't let this ruin your future. You seem to be a very nice girl."

"You know what, Marky," I stated as I ran the knife back and forth across my wrist, "I think I'm going to kill myself."

"No, Sabrina, don't do it. I'm coming right over," Marky yelled in a tone of voice as if he were actually expecting me to tell him that I was going to kill myself. Marky slammed down the phone.

I held the knife in my hand, negotiating with myself whether I should slit my wrist or not. Still holding the knife, I began to cry, and ask myself why was I ever born. After about fifteen minutes of negotiating with myself, the front door flew open. I could hear someone running towards the back of the house, into the kitchen where I was sitting with the knife in my hand rocking back and forth. It was Marky. Apparently Sheba did not Slam-lock the door when she left the house.

"Sabrina, put the knife down," he screamed as he lunged towards me and snatched the knife out of my hand. "This is crazy," exclaimed Marky, "I'm going to call 911."

"No, please don't do that. I'm going over to my mother's house. I will be okay."

"Sabrina, I'm not going to let you leave this house until you promise me that you will not kill yourself."

"I promise." I was starting to feel like I had developed another personality. Just one minute ago, I was planning to slit my wrist. While talking with Marky, I was a "level-headed" person. Was I going crazy?

"Sabrina, let me drive you over to your mother's house."

I slowly got up off of the wooden chair. Marky took hold of my arm, and led me to the front door, as if I were a helpless person who could not find her way home.

The ride to my mother's house was very quick. I was able to give Marky the shortcut streets to take, despite the negative state of mind that I was experiencing. As I was getting out of the vehicle, Marky gave me a military handshake. I was glad to be back at my mother's house. In a sense, I still felt as if what had happened between Keno and I was all a bad dream. I was hoping that I'd wake up and everything would be perfect between Keno and I.

Eight days passed by since I had spoken to Keno. I never told my mother that I had thoughts of killing myself. I only told her what I wanted her to know. I told her that we decided not to stay together, because we had different ideas about how we should plan our future. I had not returned calls that Sheba had made to me, all week. I had purposely made myself unavailable to family, friends and classmates. I was avoiding everyone. I preferred to stay at home. The only time that I saw sunlight was when I went to classes.

On one dreary Thursday evening, I decided to call Keno. I needed to speak to him. I needed to see his face. As I picked up the telephone, I began to recall the good times that Keno and I shared together. I wanted to relive those times again. I dialed the number, hoping that he would answer the phone. Finally, after the phone rang about four times, Keno picked up the phone.

"Hello."

"Hi, Keno, this is Sabrina. I need to see you."

"For what?" Keno angrily replied. "I thought I told you that it was over."

I began to feel as if I were in a desperate state.

"I know, but I just need to see you. I'm not trying to make you do anything that you don't want to do. I just need to see you."

"Marky told me that you tried to hurt yourself."

"No, I wasn't going to do it. I was just feeling very upset at the time. I'm still upset, but I think that if I see you, I would feel much better."

"Okay," Keno replied. "Where are you, at your mother's?"

"Yes," I replied.

"I'm just telling you, Sabrina, I'm going to come talk to you, but I can't stay long. I'm only doing this because you want me to."

I wanted to scream after I heard Keno's words. I felt like someone had just thrown an arrow into my heart. I felt betrayed.

"Sabrina, I'm going to drive in front of your mother's house. Please be in front of the building in twenty minutes."

"Okay," I replied.

Fifteen minutes had passed by. I decided to go downstairs and wait for Keno in front of the building. After ten minutes of waiting, I noticed Keno driving up to the building where I was standing. Keno was not driving his car. I was surprised to see him driving a new car, a shiny new grey sports car. The front of the car had headlights that resembled human eyes. He waved, capturing my attention, in order to confirm that it was he who was actually driving the vehicle that was foreign to me.

When we were together, as I recalled, he never had any plans to buy a new vehicle. As he approached where I was standing, I walked over to the passenger's side seat, and got into the vehicle. The car had a clean fresh smell, just like it was brand new. I glanced out of the window, hoping that Keno did not notice the tears that were in my eyes.

"So, hello Sabrina, how have you been? We can sit here and talk. I only have a few minutes."

"Keno, I really can't understand why we're not together."

"Sabrina, I gave you a chance. I thought that you really loved me."

"So, Keno, you wait until we break up and for celebration purposes, you buy a new car?" I angrily questioned as I inspected the back seat of the car.

"Sabrina, I had plans to buy this vehicle for us. I was just waiting for us to move in together, into our own apartment. Since our relationship didn't work out, I just decided to purchase it early."

For some strange reason, something just didn't sound sincere. At this point I didn't elaborate about Keno's explanation nor care about Keno purchasing the car. I just wanted Keno to give our relationship another chance.

"Keno, I still love you. I want us to be together."

"Sabrina, we could never rekindle our relationship. I've moved on with my life. I have other things that I'm doing with my life," he abruptly stated as he glanced at his watch, as if he were late for a dental appointment. At this point, I was so hurt that I didn't even respond. We sat in the vehicle silent for about ten minutes, until Keno broke the silence.

"Well, Sabrina, I need to be on my way."

I wanted to ask him where he was going, but instead I cooperated.

"Okay, Keno," I replied, as I quickly exited the car. I slammed the door, vowing never to look back. I felt like I had no control over what happened, and what was happening. I went upstairs into my room, and turned on the television. As I laid my head down on the pillow, the phone rang. It was Sheba.

"Hi, Sabrina, where you been girl?" she asked in her familiar Jamaican country accent.

"Well, Sheba," I've been taking it easy, and studying for my finals."

"Sabrina, I'm tired of you being depressed and moping all of the time. You have also been avoiding me. I know what I'm going to do. I'm going to contact your father, Mr. Barnes. I still have his number at the barber shop. I'm going to ask him if he would pay your way to come with me in August to Jamaica to visit my family. I'm going for two weeks."

"No, Sheba, really, that's okay. I don't feel like traveling nor being around people," I softly stated.

Sheba yelled, "You need to get away from Staten Island for awhile. You need a change of scenery. Keno has put a lot of stress on you. I think that you need to get away so that you could relax and calm your nerves. I'm going to call your father, Mr. Barnes." Before I could respond, Sheba had already hung up the phone. I really didn't want my father to know my business concerning Keno and I. Although I didn't spend a lot of time with my father, he was still supportive, whenever I did.

Shortly after I spoke with Sheba, the telephone rang again. It was my father, Mr. Barnes, who was on the phone.

"Hi, Sabrina, your friend Sheba called me, and she told me that you and your fiancée Keno broke up. He certainly was an expert on getting straight to the point. "How are you feeling?"

"I'm okay," I replied in a monotone voice.

49

"Sheba and I spoke about your going to Jamaica, West Indies with her in order to visit her family. We both know that you would benefit greatly if you went away with her for two weeks. Sheba told me how much it would cost for you to travel with her. I would love to pay for you to go."

I really was not in the mood to speak to my father about Keno. Neither was I interested in going away with Sheba to Jamaica. I didn't want to hurt my father's feelings, since his heart was set on helping me deal with Keno and I breaking up. I realized that he was only expressing concern for the trauma that I was experiencing, so I decided to accept his heartfelt offer.

"Okay, dad, I will go to Jamaica with Sheba."

"Sabrina, I want you to hold your head up high. Don't be ashamed. You can use this experience in order to push forward, and become successful in life. Don't worry, one day you will meet the right man who will appreciate you for who you are, and what you believe in."

"Thanks, dad, I really appreciate your support."

"Okay, Sabrina, you are very welcome. I will make arrangements with Sheba to pay for your airfare and hotel."

As I hung up the phone I began to picture in my mind what the island of Jamaica would look like. I pictured vibrant palm trees, blowing in the warm air. I imagined the beautiful waves in the water, glistening under the blue skies. Although I was beginning to look forward to putting Keno behind me, and stepping out into my new world, I was ready to suppress all of the hurt that I was feeling and pretend as if all of this never happened. I planned to use the vacation with Sheba as an escape from the pain, and the reality of Keno and I breaking up. I was becoming desperate to get away, so that I could purposely remove anything that reminded me of Keno. I started to pack my suitcase for my trip to Jamaica.

A week already passed since I had spoken to Sheba or my father. I was finally starting to feel less anxiety regarding Keno. It was a cloudy Sunday morning when I decided to call Sheba.

"Hi, Sheba, this is Sabrina. Did you speak to my father, Mr. Barnes, again regarding the vacation?"

"Yes, Sabrina, as a matter of fact, I was going to call you tonight, in order to tell you that your father paid for your airfare and hotel. He told me to tell you that he sent one thousand dollars for your spending money via Western Union."

"Wow," I exclaimed. "That is a lot of money." I started picturing myself further away from the pain of breaking up with Keno. "Well, Sheba, when are we leaving?"

"We are scheduled to leave in two weeks, on August 4th. The flight will be leaving the airport at 7:00 in the morning. We should reach Jamaica by 9:30 in the morning."

"I will continue to pack my bags. Mom also thinks that it would be a great idea if I went away for awhile."

"Sabrina, we are going to have a great time. My family would be happy to meet you."

"Well, Sheba, now that classes are over, I'm even more excited about our vacation. I will call you later."

The days began to quickly pass by, bringing us closer to the date of our trip to Jamaica. The day of our getaway had finally arrived. It was a very humid Sunday morning, when Sheba and I met at the airport. I had packed my nicest summer outfits along with the best sandals that I had owned. The taxi ride to the airport went by quicker than I had imagined. As I approached the airport I noticed the huge planes taking off into the sky, which reminded me of a miracle. The enormous size of the planes prompted me to praise man for inventing the formula to safely fly a machine that large and complex around the world. I was looking forward to flying away on the plane, even though I was going to unfamiliar territory. At this point, I was willing to take any risk of getting away, and forgetting about Keno.

Sheba and I were enjoying the flight to Jamaica. We watched several movies, and enjoyed a full course meal. Finally, we arrived at the Montego Bay airport. As we departed the plane, women dressed in fancy skirts gave us each a glass of rum punch and welcomed us to the island of Jamaica.

"Wow, Sheba," I exclaimed, "this is even more beautiful than I had ever imagined."

The weather was quite warm, and the people appeared as if they did not have a care in the world. The deep blue reflection of the ocean made my eyes tear. The sun beamed down on my light-brown streaked hair, as we walked towards the taxi-stand.

"Taxi-driver," stated Sheba, in her well-known country Jamaican accent, "we need a ride into town. We would like to go to the Jamaica Inn."

"Okay," the driver politely replied, "that will cost you forty U.S. dollars."

As we got into the taxi, and packed our luggage into the trunk of the vehicle, I began to wonder how this visit to Jamaica would turn out, after all. The ride to the hotel was pleasant. The driver told us jokes for most of the ride. It was obvious that he wanted to make us happy. I noticed the cows grazing along the countryside. The oceans were so beautiful. Only an imagination could actually interpret their rhythms. The palm trees that were withered as a result of the Gilbert storm peacefully blew in the trade winds. I felt as if I were in paradise.

During the first week of our vacation, Sheba and I enjoyed many water sports, going dancing, relaxing at the beach, and meeting her cousins who lived on the island. I was not thinking about Keno, at least while I was in Jamaica. I felt as if I had successfully forgotten about all of the pain and hurt that Keno had caused me. We had one more week to spend in Jamaica. I was having the time of my life.

One Tuesday afternoon, while we were out shopping, Sheba decided to take me to meet her Aunt Dora at work. It was quite a long walk from the shopping area. The rays of the sun made me feel faint. Finally, we approached the restaurant. "The Rapids Restaurant" read the tapered neon sign that hung above the front window. As we approached the front entrance of the restaurant, a young man, who appeared to be in his mid-thirties, greeted us.

"Come in; welcome to the Rapids. You may be seated anywhere you like. Make yourself at home."

Sheba and I picked a cozy seat facing the front entrance. The décor of the restaurant reminded me of the funk era of the 1970's.

"Hi, waiter," stated Sheba, as she put the menu into the center of the wicker table, "I'm looking for my Aunt Dora; she works here. Would you be kind enough to check and see if she's here now?"

"Oh, Dora, that's your auntie? She's a nice woman. She makes me laugh a lot. She has a good sense of humor. Look here, let me go and check. Me soon come back."

After about five minutes, a woman abruptly walked up to our table. She was a fair-skinned woman with black and grey Shirley Temples in her hair. She seemed quite friendly and spoke with a soft voice. She wore a white dress with a pink scarf around her neck.

"Sheba," the woman exclaimed as she tightly hugged Sheba. "So how's life in the States?"

"Life is good," replied Sheba, "this is my best friend, Sabrina. Sabrina, this is my Aunt Dora."

"Pleased to meet you, Sabrina," Dora stated as she mysteriously glanced towards the front door.

"I brought Sabrina to our hometown so that she could have some fun."

"Oh, don't worry, darling, you will have fun while you're here, because here in Jamaica, there's no problem." We all chuckled. We sat together for awhile talking about our plans for the upcoming week. As we were talking, I noticed a handsome young man waiting on a table not far from where we were seated. I was almost distracted by his smile. He had the prettiest smile that I had ever seen. He wore a blue dress shirt, with dark trousers. He was sporting the same fade haircut that Keno wore. He also had the same gleam in his eyes that Keno had when I first met him. I noticed that he had been watching me, and we had caught each other's eye several times. I felt the urgency to meet him up close, and personal so I decided to speak up.

"Sheba, do you see that guy over there?" I stated as I pointed over towards the kitchen area of the restaurant.

"Yes, why?" Sheba replied.

"I just have to meet him," I cheerfully shouted.

"Oh," Dora hastily interrupted, "that's Gary. He's a real nice guy. A lot of girls out here like him, but he nah give dem no play."

"Tell him to come here," I desperately demanded. As Dora and Gary were walking over towards the table where Sheba and I were seated, I began to feel butterflies in my stomach. Although I was very nervous, I pretended that I was calm.

"Gary, I want you to meet Sabrina. Sabrina, this is Gary."

"Hi, Gary."

"Hello, Sabrina, pleased to meet you," he politely replied as he rubbed the side of his face. "Sabrina, come over here and sit with me for a minute," Gary demanded. "I want to talk with you." Gary swiftly led me to the other side of the room to a table that was far away from the front door of the restaurant. "So, Sabrina, how long have you been in Jamaica? Is this your first time here?"

"Well," I replied, "I have been here for a week. I came to visit the island with my best friend, over there," I replied as I pointed towards the direction of where Sheba and her Aunt Dora were comfortably seated. "This is my first time visiting the island."

"You look very nice, Sabrina. I was watching you since you came into the restaurant," Gary exclaimed in a loud, but appealing Jamaican accent. "Sabrina, where are you staying, in town, or in the country. If you didn't know, this side of town is called the country."

"We're staying at the Jamaica Inn, not too far from here. I guess you can say that we're staying in the country." We both laughed.

"Well, Sabrina, I live in the part of Jamaica that we call the country. I live on this side of town, not too far from here. How about if I stop by, maybe tomorrow after work, about six o'clock?"

"That would be great," I cheerfully replied. "When you come to the hotel, just ask for Sabrina, Sabrina Matheson."

"Okay, I will see you on tomorrow night. It was nice talking with you, Sabrina. I see the boss coming; I'd better be leaving." I was desperate to receive confirmation for Gary coming to visit me at the hotel on tomorrow. I felt the urgency to question him.

"So, Gary, are you sure that you will come to visit me on tomorrow?"

"Yeah, man, don't worry, be happy. I'm definitely coming to see you." Although we didn't exchange telephone numbers, for some reason I was satisfied with his promise. Gary was someone that I could fall in love with, I thought. I decided to crown him as my new king. The thought of him being my king was exciting. He was different. He spoke with an accent. He was gentle. He was Jamaican.

The evening that Gary had promised to meet me at the hotel finally arrived. Sheba and I were talking about our junior high school days, and eating a snack. Suddenly, there was a loud knock on the door.

"Who is it?" Sheba exclaimed.

"It's Gary," replied the individual at the door. Before Sheba could turn around, I was there, reaching for the doorknob, in order to let Gary in.

"Come in, have a seat, Gary," I demanded. Gary had on a colorful shirt, with a pair of white trousers. He had on an attractive cologne, which reminded me of Keno. He also had the gleam in his eyes, the same gleam that I noticed on the day that I met him. It was the same gleam that Keno had in his eyes. I was determined not to allow the reminders of Keno prevent me from getting to know Gary. As Gary entered the room, Sheba pretended to make herself occupied with different books that she had in the drawer.

"So, hi Gary, you did keep your word about coming to visit me."

"Yes," he exclaimed as he showed off his pearly, white smile, "I told you that I would visit, and I kept my word."

Gary and I began to spend most of the time together during the last four days of our stay in Jamaica. We visited many of his relatives, went out to dinner, and visited the beach. It was finally time for Sheba and I to go back home. It was a bright, sunny Sunday morning when Gary met us at the airport in Montego Bay. He had expressed that he wanted to see us off to New York, and conversate while we waited for our flight to leave the island.

"Sabrina," Gary politely asked, "how did you like your visit to Jamaica?"

"I loved it," I exclaimed in a loud voice, as if I were announcing it to the universe. "Like we discussed on last evening, I'm going to come back in October to visit you."

"I would be looking forward to seeing you again, Sabrina." Spending time with Gary made me feel important again. He gave me all of the attention that I missed, since breaking up with Keno.

"So you two love birds are going to see each other real soon, eh?" Sheba questioned in her famous motherly-tone of voice.

"Yes," Gary replied, "she's my special one. I'm looking forward to seeing her again."

Before we knew it, the time had come for us to board the airplane. Gary promised that he would call, and I did the same. Sheba and I could see Gary standing at the waving stand at the airport, as we sat, waiting for our flight to leave the runway. As our flight ascended into the air, I began to feel as if I had accomplished something great. I had met someone who really cared about me, and enjoyed spending quality time with me. Gary made me feel special again. I was looking forward to seeing him again.

Two weeks had passed by since I came back home from Jamaica. It was a warm day in September. I had just began my senior year in college. I was getting ready for my two o'clock class, when the telephone rang.

"Hello."

"Hi, this is the New York telephone operator, I have a collect call from Gary; would you accept?"

"Yes, I will. Hello, hello," I exclaimed.

"Hi, Sabrina," this is Gary. "How are you doing, my special one?"

"I'm fine; I miss you."

"I miss you too," Gary replied.

"I'm preparing to go to my class. Remember, I told you that I would be graduating from college in May, right?"

"Yes, Sabrina, I remember you telling me, and I did promise you that I'd be there. My father filed for me to come to Canada to live with him. He told me that the paperwork should be ready by sometime in April."

"That's good. I would love to have you present. It would make me so happy."

"Sabrina, when I come up there, I'm going to take good care of you. I will pay the rent, and treat you really nice." Gary's words made me feel like I could conquer the world. His words were the temporary relief for the pain that I had felt as a result of Keno and I breaking up.

"So, Gary, I'm on my way out; you can call me later on." As I proceeded to grab my books, the phone rang again. It was my father, Mr. Barnes. I had not spoken to him about the vacation yet. I did speak to my mother, and I told her about my meeting Gary. Surprisingly, she had no opinion at all concerning Gary, not to mention his collect calls being billed to her phone. I wasn't certain of my father's reaction to my telling him about Gary, but it was worth a shot.

"Hello, Sabrina, how are you? I figured that I'd give you a few days to settle in before I called you in order to ask about your getaway to Jamaica. So, how was your trip?"

"It was very nice," I reluctantly replied. "I met most of Sheba's family. They were really nice. We went to the beach, and shopping. We had a nice time."

"So who's this guy Larry or something, that you met in Jamaica? Your mom told me earlier when I had called for you."

"Oh, Gary. He's a nice guy that I met."

"Sabrina, let me tell you something. I did not send you to Jamaica to bring back a souvenir that could cost you your life."

"Oh, no, dad, it's not that serious." My father was unstoppable with his words. He was determined to get his point across.

58

"Sabrina, you done went to the bottom of the barrel. I mean if you want a husband you could find one from America. Don't make me feel like I've made a mistake, when I thought that I was helping you, by sending you on vacation," he pleaded. It was obvious that he and my mother talked about the situation. I figured that I would just play it cool.

"No, dad, don't worry, he's just a friend."

"Okay, I'm just letting you know, as a man, you need to take your time. Don't go having kids, because I'm telling you, this man that you met does not want any responsibilities." My father was talking like he actually knew Gary.

Gary and I wrote many letters, and sent cards with pictures to each other. We spoke to each other every day. Gary had sent me a nice pair of gold earrings in the mail. I went to visit him in Jamaica during the months of October and November. We spent intimate times together, and enjoyed evenings out on the town. I began to feel like a brand new person. I was in love with Gary. He began to become the center of my life. When I learned that Keno got married to someone else, it did not bother me. I began to mentally paint pictures of Gary in the compartments of my mind. Gary was constantly assuring me that he would be present at my graduation in May.

One day, I decided to go shopping at the Big Apple Bazaar in order to pick out a bracelet and a few shirts for Gary. On my way, north of the Bazaar, I walked past a booth. I felt as if a magnet pulled me back. I looked up and noticed a sign which read "Spiritual Readings by Mrs. Mary." I was always told as a child that one should stay away from people who perform readings. Our family Pentecostal religion preached against getting involved with such influences. I was very curious. I began to feel helpless. I quickly walked into the booth and noticed a woman sitting in a bamboo-wicker chair. She appeared to be a charming, young, pale-faced woman with long black hair. Her eyes gleamed with the glow of deep green candles. The aroma of the booth reminded me of freshly-picked rose petals. Her entire presence was almost magical. She must have known that I was new to this world. As I reached out my hand and curiously touched one of the crystals that were placed on the table nearby where she was sitting, she began to lure me into her trap. It was as if the predator had mystically mastered the prey.

"Hello, sweetie, have a seat," she slyly commanded, "you need a reading."

"What does that mean," I replied in a soft voice.

"You need me to tell you your future. There is a lot of evil around you." After that statement, I was convinced that she was telling the truth.

"How much do you charge?"

"Only twenty-five dollars." I felt as if I were being intimidated. I almost felt helpless. I reached into my wallet and handed her the twenty-five dollars.

"Okay," she stated as she pulled out a deck of cards from the drawer. As she was shuffling the cards, I began to notice strange looking cards. I have never seen any cards like such in my life. There were cards with the faces of a devil, some cards with angels, and many other distinctive-looking cards.

"Pick seven," she stated as she mysteriously glanced into my eyes. "Wow, who's the guy that you just met? I see a new relationship. Is he overseas?"

"Yes," I replied.

"He's very sick," she yelled as she added seven more cards to the pile of cards that were already on the table. "It looks like somebody gave him poison to drink which caused him to have problems with his stomach. Looks like a lady did it. Many women like him. She wants to be his wife. She tried to trap him. Something's going on with his visa. Is he trying to get here?"

"Yes," I replied, "his father filed for him. He's just waiting to hear from the embassy." During the entire time sitting there listening to her, I was literally being spooked trying to figure out how she knew this information.

"What's your name, sweetie?" she asked in a luring monotone voice.

"Sabrina."

"Okay, Sabrina, I can help you. I can help you get Gary here to America faster. I can also help you keep Gary to yourself. I will also help him with his stomach problem."

I was so elated. This woman was telling me exactly what I wanted to hear. She made my day.

"Sabrina, I will start all of the work for two hundred dollars. You can give me one hundred now, and come back on next Sunday with the balance. Sabrina, take this red candle. I want you to write your name one time on it, and Gary's name next to yours. Light the candle for fifteen minutes for five nights." I reached into my wallet and quickly handed her five twenty dollar bills. She aggressively began to explain the spiritual plans that she had for Gary.

"Thank you, Mrs. Mary," I exclaimed. I started to believe that Mrs. Mary was my best friend. I trusted her. I could not wait to leave the Big Apple Bazaar so that I could call Gary and tell him what the Tarot card reader told me. Was Gary really a sick man? Were there really that many women that wanted his attention? Could she really help me get him into the country quicker, so that he would be at my graduation? I had to believe her. She was the only one that was helping me to live my fantasy about being together with Gary. I was convinced that once I burned the red candle that she gave me, Gary would not be attracted to the women in Jamaica who wanted his attention. The money that I gave her was nothing compared to what could happen if I did not cooperate with her. I quickly returned to the counter and paid for the bracelet, shirts and cologne that I picked out for Gary. I could not wait to contact him.

When I reached home, I could not wait to drop the packages. I rushed over to the telephone, and dialed Gary's number.

"Gary, guess what? While I was out shopping for a few things for you, I went to a Tarot card reader." Gary was silent. "She told me that somebody gave you poison to drink and that as a result, you are having a lot of problems with your stomach. She also told me that she could help the process of your visa for Canada come through quicker. She told me that she could help you with your stomach, too." I refused to tell him about the women who wanted to be his wife. I would handle that separately.

"Wow, Sabrina, who is this woman?" She's absolutely correct. I have been having a lot of problems with my stomach. I've been sick for a while, but I did not want to tell you. I even threw up on several occasions while you were down here, but I did not tell you. I have been to many doctors, but they all tell me that there's nothing wrong. I even let them put the tube down into my stomach, but they found nothing. My sister even took my jacket to a reader here in Jamaica, and they told her the same thing."

"Oh, my goodness, Gary," I instantly felt the obligation to help him get well. "Don't worry, Ms. Mary guaranteed me that she would help you. She also guaranteed me that she would speed up the process of you getting your visa to Canada. Just think about it, Gary, you coming to America, and we'll be together. You will also get help with your stomach. Ms. Mary told me to come back on Sunday so that I could get a candle to burn so that your visa papers would be processed faster. She is also giving me a candle and bath so that your stomach would feel better. She told me that I have to give her some more money so that she could start the work. Ms. Mary said that when you come to America she will cure your stomach condition."

"Oh, Sabrina, you really are my special one. I love you."

"I love you too, Gary."

"Oh, Sabrina, my special one, when I move to Canada, I want you to come visit me at my father's house, okay?"

"No problem." We both laughed. Shortly after we spoke, I went to the post office, and mailed Gary his bracelet, shirts, and cologne. I was happy again. Gary needed me.

I went back to the Big Apple Bazaar in order to see Ms. Mary. She appeared very happy to see me.

"Hi, Sabrina," she stated as she sipped on a tall glass of water.

"Hi, Ms. Mary. I came to drop off the hundred dollars to contribute to the work that you are doing for Gary."

"Sabrina, I went to the gods last night and they told me that I have to charge you one thousand dollars for the work that I need to do for you. I will take the hundred, but you will owe me a balance of nine hundred." I was guessing that the hundred dollars that I gave her on last week was just a bonus.

"Well, Ms. Mary, I was not expecting to spend so much money today. I'm still a student and I don't have much cash around."

"Well," she angrily replied, "can't you go to your credit cards, borrow it, or apply for a loan?" Ms. Mary obviously wasn't concerned about how I got the money, she just wanted it. Her very presence intimidated me. Who were the "gods" that she spoke about? The mystery in her words made me anxious and fearful. I would find the money out of fear and intimidation.

"Okay, Ms. Mary, I will be back on tomorrow with the balance." The strange look in her eyes was a warning to me, but I had no other option, but to bring her the money. I called Sheba and five other people that I had not spoken to in months, in order to borrow the money that I needed for Ms. Mary. It was a stressful task, but I finally raised the money. I went back to Ms. Mary on the following week and gave her the nine hundred dollars.

"Don't worry, Sabrina, I'm going to help you. Gary will be here in no time. Do you trust me?" she asked in a sly, but convincing tone of voice.

"Yes, I do."

"Here, Sabrina, take these crystals home with you and this incense cone. Put the crystals under the pillow before you pray, and light the cone incense."

"Thank you, Ms. Mary, I will let you know when Gary comes to the States."

"Be sure to bring him here, so that I can finish helping him. Gary will call you sometime in April and will tell you that he's on his way to Canada to live; trust me, Sabrina."

During the month of March, Gary and I spoke on the phone, and wrote letters to each other more than ever. One day, during the first week of April, Gary telephoned me.

"Sabrina, guess what, my visa is ready. I will be moving to Canada on next week."

"That is wonderful. See, Gary, Ms. Mary is really doing a great job helping us." "The only problem that I'm having is with my stomach, replied Gary."

"Don't worry, Gary, you will be with me in New York, soon. She will help you. I already paid for the work."

"Sabrina, I want to see you. Here's the information, where my father lives. I would like you to meet me there in Canada."

"That would be great." Gary gave me the information. I would work out my schedule, even if I were to meet him for only three days.

I booked a round trip flight to Ontario, Canada. The flight to Canada was comfortable, and quick. After the flight landed, I looked for a taxi. As one approached I got into the back seat.

"Hello, I would like to go to 122 Sandpipe Road." As the taxi drove up to the house, I noticed Gary and a man who appeared quite older than him standing on the porch. They were expecting, and waiting for my arrival.

As I stepped out of the taxi, Gary ran up to the car, and grabbed my luggage out of the trunk.

"Hello, Sabrina," he shouted, as I paid the driver the fare for my ride. "This is my father, Bob. Bob, this is my girlfriend, Sabrina from New York."

"Hi, Sabrina," stated his father as he abruptly shook my hand. "Come inside, and make yourself comfortable, Sabrina."

As I stepped into the house, I noticed a lot of plants placed against the entire back wall of the living room. The furniture in the living room reminded me of a royal palace. The aroma of freshly lit incense intensely overpowered the perfume that I was wearing. On that evening Gary and I enjoyed a well-prepared Jamaican dinner at his father's home. Three days had already passed by. Gary and I enjoyed the sights of Toronto, Canada. We spent a lot of time dancing at the clubs, going to the movies, and bowling.

On one evening before going to bed, Gary asked me to come into the basement in order to talk to him. I found that to be quite odd, since we had never spent time together in that area of the house since I'd been visiting.

"Sabrina, so how are you enjoying yourself so far?" Gary asked.

"Fine, I really like it here. It's much different from New York."

All of a sudden, almost out of the blue sky, Gary punched me in the side of my face.

"Why did you do that?" I angrily asked. "Get away from me," I shouted as I ran upstairs.

"What happened?" exclaimed Gary's father Bob.

"Gary just threw a punch in my face, for no reason." As I finished my sentence, Gary ran upstairs after me.

"I'm sorry Sabrina, please forgive me." "I don't know what happened to me." Although I was still in a state of shock, trying to figure out why Gary struck me, I forgave him.

It was finally time for me to go back home to New York. Gary arranged my transportation to the airport. The flight home was very quick and comfortable.

I had no problem getting back into the swing of going to my classes. Besides, the special month was quickly approaching. I was looking forward to graduating in May, and of course having Gary here in town.

It was a cool, breezy day in the beginning of the month of May, when Gary telephoned me with good news. "Hi, Sabrina, my special one, how are you today?"

"I'm better now that I'm hearing your voice."

"I wanted you to know that I will be in New York to visit you in two weeks. Isn't it great? I will be able to come to your graduation, just like I promised you. As long as I have my visa, I can travel to New York." I was excited, but at the same time speechless.

The day that Gary came to New York finally approached. I had made arrangements to pick Gary up from the airport in Newark, New Jersey. As Gary entered into the waiting area of the Air Canada flights,

I greeted him with a hug. "Hi, Gary," I exclaimed. "It's a pleasure finally meeting with you on American soil." We both laughed, as Gary kissed me on the cheek.

I enjoyed giving Gary a tour of New York, and pointing out famous landmarks during our cab ride back to Staten Island. We finally reached back to my apartment. When Gary had previously told me that he was coming to New York, I had made arrangements to rent a beautiful studio apartment. I had also landed an evening job counseling troubled teens at the local group home which paid my bills, and allowed me to enjoy extra leisure activities.

"So, Sabrina, this is a very nice apartment."

"Thanks, Gary, you can just put your suitcase down over there," I stated as I pointed to the oversized closet located near the front door. Gary seemed a little suspicious, and almost cynical as he sat at the kitchen table. He began making facial gestures, as if he had a hidden agenda regarding something, or someone. I didn't make a big deal about it. Although he was a stranger, I made up my mind that I would treat him as if I'd known him for years. Gary and I spent a lot of time together going to the movies, and meeting up with some of my family and old acquaintances.

Gary kept his word. On May 23rd, he attended my graduation from Wagner College. It was a very exciting day.

A week following my graduation, it was time for Gary to go back to Canada. "Well, Sabrina, it's time for me to go back home on the day after tomorrow." All of a sudden, I began to feel as if I had just lost my best friend. I was not satisfied with hearing what Gary was saying. Gary was the only person that I had to keep me company. I was determined to make him an offer that he could not refuse.

"Gary," I exclaimed, "we could get married, so that you would not have to go back home. If we get married, the Immigration Department will not harass you about going back to Canada."

All of a sudden, Gary's face lit up like a light bulb. "Oh, Sabrina," Gary shouted, "that would be a great idea."

"Gary, we can go down to the Justice of the Peace, and they will perform the ceremony. I will ask my mother and my aunt to be witnesses. We'll go down there in two days, in order to get the information."

"Sabrina, what about us meeting with Ms. Mary, the reader? Remember, you said that she would help me with my stomach?"

"Oh, yeah," I casually replied. I almost forgot. As a matter of fact, let us go down to the Big Apple Bazaar in order to meet her, on today." I called a taxi in order to take us to meet Ms. Mary.

As we got out of the taxi, Gary put his hand on his stomach and made gestures, as if he were attempting to vomit. "Excuse me, Sabrina, I'm very sorry. My stomach is in a lot of pain."

"Don't worry," I replied, "we're going inside to see Ms. Mary, who can help you."

As we approached the booth where Ms. Mary was seated, I noticed several statues of saints in the front. It was almost as if they were greeting us. There was a statue of Mary, Michael The Archangel, and others that I've never seen before. As I pulled the curtain back, in anticipation of seeing Ms. Mary, she was seated in her royal seat, surrounded by white candles. The incense burned with a strong scent of sweet candy. Ms. Mary appeared as if she were expecting our visit. Her mystical eyes gave me a chill as she greeted me. "Hi, Sabrina, I was wondering when you were going to bring him to me."

As Gary and I sat in the two chairs positioned directly in front of where she was seated, I proceeded to introduce her to Gary. "Ms. Mary, this is Gary, from Jamaica."

"Hi, Gary, it's a pleasure to meet you," she stated as she glanced over to the window. "So, Gary, I have been helping Sabrina with your visa. It's because of me that you were able to get to America so quickly. I have also been praying to the gods for you, concerning the issue with your stomach. You know that someone—a lady—gave you something to drink. It should have killed you by "now," but I've been doing extra prayers for you, which saved you. "Now," stated Ms. Mary as she turned over seven cards from a deck of cards, "I'm looking into your belly. It is very black. I can get it out, but the gods are telling me that it's going to cost you five thousand U.S. dollars. They're telling me that I have to go to the graveyard to do the work."

I could not believe what I was hearing. Gary was reacting like he was used to receiving predictions regarding his life. This type of information was all new to me. Ms. Mary quoted five thousand dollars as if it were one dollar. I was eager to interject but before I could, Gary interrupted.

"I'm so happy, Ms. Mary," Gary shouted in his country Jamaican accent. "When Sabrina told me that you told her the condition about my stomach, I couldn't believe it. It was as if I were dreaming. I went everywhere in Jamaica for help, and spent so much money, and nobody could help me."

"Well, you'd better be thankful for me," she exclaimed. "I am the one who could take this spell off of you. Somebody did witchcraft to you—an evil spell. I am the one who will reverse it with my witchcraft. I'm not like these other spiritual people that you see around. I am an Israelite," Ms. Mary exclaimed, as she cast her mystical eyes on the both of us. "You just bring me at least three thousand dollars so that I can start the work," she demanded. Both Gary and I thanked her for her help. "Before you go, take these candles, one white you burn at night-time, and the red one, burn during the day for good luck. Gary, you eat these peanuts. Take about a handful of these each morning for five days. It will help you with the gas and bloating that you are experiencing."

As we were walking out of the Bazaar Gary exclaimed, "How did she know that I had gas and bloating? I never told her." We both laughed. I began to feel as if finally, my life was back on track. I was getting married, and we had somebody who was helping us with Gary's problem. We weren't worried about raising the money for Ms. Mary.

Two days later we went to Borough Hall. We obtained all of the information. I decided to pay the fee, and get our marriage over with. I called my mother and told her the good news. "Hi, Mom, Gary and I are down here at Borough Hall. We need a witness, because we are going to get married right away."

"Sabrina, I know that at the graduation you were briefly speaking about the possibility, but are you sure that this is what you want to do?

"Yes," I replied.

"Okay, well, if this is that you want, your Aunt Debbie and I will meet you both down at Borough Hall in order to be witnesses."

My mother and aunt met Gary and I at Borough Hall. Gary and I were finally married. Gary's family in Canada were not too happy about him not coming back to Canada, but we didn't care. I introduced Gary to my landlord, who was a director for a large insurance agency in New York City. He was able to introduce us to an immigration lawyer who handled Gary's green card paperwork. My landlord appointed Gary with a full time position working in the insurance office with overtime, paid vacation, and medical benefits. Gary didn't believe it, but he was blessed.

It was time for me to apply for my new job with the local utility company. We finally saved up two thousand dollars, when we decided to go visit Ms. Mary. Ms. Mary had the usual mystical look on her face. "Oh, come in, sit down," she stated in a tone of victory.

"We have so much to tell you," I exclaimed. "Gary and I got married, and he got a really great job. I'm about to apply for the job that the college offered me."

"Well," replied Ms. Mary, "I hope that you both realize that it is because of me. I am the one that is helping the both of you," she angrily stated. "I'm doing all of this work, and I'm not getting any money from you."

"Ms. Mary, we have two thousand dollars of the money that you requested. If you can help us, we can pay the balance off over time."

"This is not a bank," she hastily replied, "but you both are young, and I will work with you. Sabrina, by the way, you're pregnant. We better get Gary healed right away. You don't want the baby to be born with this bad luck that Gary has."

By now, I was more than afraid. I was terrified. I quickly gave Ms. Mary the two thousand dollars, which were all hundred dollar bills. We all went into the back of the area where Ms. Mary was practicing her magic. She held a jar of warm water that was sealed.

"Gary, now you put your hand on top of my hand as we shake this water up and down." They both had their hands on the jar, shaking it up and down. "Harder, shake the jar harder," she shouted as Gary desperately followed her command. Finally, after about forty desperate shakes of the jar of water, a huge, thick black smog entered into the jar. It was almost as if someone poured tar into the water.

"Wow," we all exclaimed.

"This black smog that you see in the jar of water is what was inside of your stomach. How do you feel?"

"I feel much better, Ms. Mary. Oh, thank you, you healed me. I don't feel the pain that was in my stomach."

"You are welcome" replied Ms. Mary. "Just don't forget that I'm the one who is helping you. Make sure that you come back with the balance of three thousand dollars, so that the bad luck won't come back. Oh, and Sabrina, take this cone of incense and candle and light the both of them together for good luck with your job."

We were both so happy. A week later I found out that I was pregnant. Gary didn't seem so happy about it, but he was a very good pretender. Gary and I decided that Ms. Mary was overcharging us, and that we would find someone else to help us. Although I was pregnant, I was able to gain a very good paying job with the local utility company.

Over the next three weeks, Gary's demeanor changed. He became very controlling, and at times physically abusive. It did not matter to him that I was pregnant with his child. He was becoming more and more unreasonable as the days went by. I was spending more time arguing and fighting with Gary than anything else. Gary began to isolate me from my family, and the few associates that I had, including my best friend Sheba.

One day, while Gary was at work during the evening, the phone rang.

"Hello."

"Hi, Sabrina, this is your father. Where have you been? What the heck is going on?"

"Well, Dad, the guy from Jamaica came here from Canada to visit, and we got married." There was brief silence before Mr. Barnes became hysterical.

"What, are you kidding me? Sabrina, you just graduated from college. What's wrong with you? You went to the bottom of the barrel with this one." Before I was able to say one word, Mr. Barnes hung up the phone.

When Gary came home from work, we agreed that we were both being spiritually fixed by Ms. Mary, and that we would find a witch from Brooklyn to help us. I was already six months pregnant with Gary

Junior. By this time we had our own vehicle. We decided to drive around Brooklyn in search of our new spiritual reader. Finally, we passed a huge building which had a sign which read "Readings by Ms. Zuma." Wow, I thought, she must be really good. We parked the vehicle in front of the shop. As we entered into the storefront, there was religious music playing, something about "Jesus will help you" and "Satan, your kingdom must come down." The store smelled like a combination of freshly scented oils. On one side of the wall there were eight ounce candles arranged by colors in glass holders. I noticed many statues of saints on display, for sale. As we approached the counter, a girl who appeared to be about fifteen years old offered to assist us.

"May I help you?"

"Yes," I replied, "we would like to speak with the reader."

"Oh, very good, she's an excellent reader, and she helps a lot of people. She is very busy right now, but if you like, you may wait."

"How much does she charge for a reading?"

"Oh, only thirty dollars."

"Okay, we'll wait."

There were many people waiting to see this so-called Ms. Zuma. As we were waiting to see her, a burst of smoke-filled incense illuminated the entire room. Gary and I began to cough. Finally, after waiting for about one hour, a short woman with a scarf tied backwards on her head appeared from behind a shrine of beads. She had on dark clothes, and had a dark complexion. She spoke with a West Indian accent. It was evident that she had her surroundings under complete control. She spoke with authority, walked with authority, and made gestures with authority. It was obvious that the girl in the front who offered to assist us feared her.

"Who's next?" the woman asked as she placed a newly-lit purple candle on the countertop.

"We are," I anxiously shouted.

As she led us into the back of the store, I began to feel spooked. There was a black chicken running around the area. There were many candles lit on the countertop. There was a deck of cards sitting on the table with a monkey's paw on display.

"So, how may I help you?" she asked in a monotone voice.

I was anxious to give her our report. "We are here because we went to a reader over in Staten Island. She said that we had to pay her five thousand U.S. dollars for helping my husband with his stomach. We gave her two thousand dollars, but we don't think that we should pay the rest. It's too much money. We also have been fighting a whole lot."

"Pick ten cards," she stated as she finished shuffling the deck of cards that was on the table. As I handed her the ten cards, she flipped them over, and frowned. "Wow, I see that this woman is robbing you. She can't help you. She's upset because she feels that you owe her money. I can help you. First, I need you to buy five different statues of saints. You have to have them in your home, in order to receive power."

I didn't mind, since Gary and I had planned on moving to a larger apartment during the next month. I would have more room.

"I also need you to buy two black pull-out candles. We have to reverse the curse that the reader that you went to before put on you both. I want you to write her name on the candle seven times. You will tell the girl up front to give you some destruction oil and power oil. You must burn these candles for fifteen minutes, twice a day. Also, you both need to take cleansing baths. You still have time. Just start off by doing this first. You can leave me two hundred dollars, and we'll take it one day at a time. Come see me in about two weeks."

I handed her the money, and proceeded to purchase the candles, oils, and five statues of saints. When we arrived into our new apartment,

I put the saints on display. Every morning and evening we prayed to the saints for direction and comfort. We also lit the candles as directed.

Gary Jr. was finally born. Gary and I began to fight every day. Gary became more verbally and physically abusive. It seemed like the more I prayed to the saints about my issues, the worse the problems became. The police came to the house many times, as a result of Gary's abusive behavior. I never had the courage to have him arrested for his actions. Gary and I continued our rituals for about a year. We prayed often to the statues, and lighted our candles. I became pregnant again, and gave birth to Rebecca.

The violence became very intense between Gary and me. I found myself paying all of the bills, even though Gary worked. One day, Gary and I decided that we needed to go back in order to visit Ms. Zuma for guidance. We brought Gary Jr. and Rebecca to my mother's house for the day.

When we arrived at Ms. Zuma's storefront, she was standing outside, as if she were expecting our arrival. "Come in, I was waiting for you to come back," she stated as she held the door open for us. As she led us to the rear of the storefront, a black rooster ran towards us. "Don't panic," she demanded. "This is what you need in your house for protection." As we sat down, Ms. Zuma began to write on a piece of paper. "I've been thinking about the both of you. I want to perform a total cleansing for you and your family. It will cost you two thousand dollars."

As I attempted to speak, Gary abruptly interrupted me, and said, "No problem. I will bring you the money next week."

I found that to be quite strange because next week was a major Holiday. We needed the money to buy food.

"Ms. Zuma, why can' t you do it this week?" questioned Gary.

"I can only do it on Saturday. You both come along with your two children. Come when the store is closed. I think that it would be fine if you came here around eight o'clock in the night. Before you come, I need you to stop off at the live poultry store and purchase two live chickens, one male and one female. Also, go to the pet store and bring me a brown male rabbit. I need these for sacrifices," Ms. Zuma exclaimed. Gary and I proceeded to leave the shop.

During the week leading up to our spiritual cleansing, Gary and I prayed diligently to the saints. A voice came to me, and told me to set up an altar with candy, donuts, red wine, and bread. I don't know who the voice represented, but I obeyed. I was also instructed to put flowers on the altar, and light a green candle for money, and a red candle for love. Each day that I checked the altar it appeared as if the wine was slowly disappearing as if someone were drinking it. The candy and bread on the altar was distributed among Gary, myself, and the children. By the time we ate the pastries, it appeared as if something or someone had sapped the flavor from everything that was on the altar. The candles on the altar burned with passion. The Caridad statue that I prayed to appeared to be crying. It was as if she felt the sudden terror that we would soon experience.

Saturday quickly arrived. Before we left in order to see Ms. Zuma, I replaced the wine, bread, and pastries onto the altar. I also lit a white candle for clearance, as instructed by the voice in my head. On our way to Zuma's shop, we stopped off at the pet shop, and bought a brown, male rabbit. We also stopped at the live poultry shop, and bought one male chicken and one female chicken.

When we arrived at Zuma's shop, she demanded that we all take off our clothes. Myself, Gary and the two children stood up naked in a tub of water that she prepared for us. "You all need thorough cleansing. This whole family is cursed. I'm going to mix a bath for all of you. Once

I'm finished, I have to pour it over your head. This will be the beginning of the cleansing. "Gary," she demanded, "give me the two thousand dollars."

After Gary handed her the money, which was twenty one hundred dollar bills, she threw it on the floor, next to the rabbit that we bought. The bath that she was mixing smelled very sweet. Gary Jr. and Rebecca began to cry. Once she finished mixing the baths, she poured the liquid over all of our heads. The bath that she gave us lasted for about one hour. Zuma gave us each a white sheet to wrap around our bodies. Zuma led us all up to the front of the storefront. She began chanting. She proceeded to light a cigar, and smoke it. Zuma commanded us all to stand up in the middle of the room. Zuma began to surround us in a circle, using white chalk. She also drew symbols of the cross and unfamiliar symbols. She began to light tall white candles, and placed them in the circle with us. Zuma put on some music, which resembled African tribal music. Zuma fell into a trance, and picked up a bottle of vodka, and began spitting the vodka onto the light of the candles. She began to foam at the mouth. Zuma proceeded to light two additional candles. These two were red.

Zuma grabbed the first chicken out of the bag. It was as if the chicken knew that her life was being sacrificed for something. Zuma gave me the female chicken and gave Gary the male chicken. Zuma commanded me, first to cut off the neck of the female chicken. Zuma handed me the knife, as she rang the large bell that she held in her hand.

"Sabrina, cut the neck." I was totally in shock, but I knew that this had to be done. I grabbed the knife into my hand and began to aggressively cut the neck of the chicken. The blood began to quickly drip out of the chicken's neck, when Zuma yelled, "Drop the blood over the candles. Drop the blood over the candles." I dripped the blood from the chicken's neck onto the candles, and threw the head onto the candle and the body remained moving on the floor. Gary proceeded to do the same thing that I did, using the male chicken. After Gary finished, Zuma took the chickens and began to rub both chickens on each of us as she chanted in an unfamiliar voice. Gary Jr. and Rebecca began to scream. After the ritual was over, Zuma rushed to put the bloody candles, and dead chickens into a bag.

"Sabrina and Gary, this bag contains the dead chickens. On your way home, drop the dead chickens at any busy intersection. Do not let anyone see you. You must hurry. Also, write what you desire for your enemies on this piece of parchment paper."

After we wrote our wish, we gave Zuma the two pieces of paper. Gary and I both watched Zuma as she aggressively stuffed the two pieces of parchment paper into the anus of the rabbit. I found it to be quite cruel, but Ms. Zuma demanded that this needed to be done. "I am going to take this rabbit with me to the cemetery," she stated. "I have a lot of work to do."

Gary and I drove off, looking for a busy intersection to throw the bags into. Finally, we approached a busy intersection. I rolled the window down on the passenger side where I was sitting.

"Now drop it," yelled Gary. I quickly dropped the bag, hoping that nobody would see me. I was happy that nobody actually saw me dropping the bag of dead chickens.

Zuma, Gary and I performed many rituals also with pigeons, in order to gain spiritual power. We practiced for at least three years. Gary and I visited Ms. Zuma every week. I found myself spending two hundred dollars or more each week buying candles, incense, and oils in order to protect myself from my enemies.

Gary and I began to have even more fights and arguments. Gary managed to cut himself with a piece of glass, call the police and claim that

I assaulted him. Of course, they arrested me. I was the individual being abused, but the abuser was able to set me up. After three days, I was released on my own recognizance. Is this what I graduated from college for? I slowly began to feel as if my self-esteem was going lower and lower as the days moved on. I found it difficult to keep steady employment, and maintain motherhood, due to the stress that I was experiencing.

I remember Ms. Zuma telling me that I had the ability to become a spiritual reader. I decided to open my own business. I made spiritual baths for my clients, and gave them spiritual readings and candles for a fee.

Gary and I began to have more, and more conflict. I began to feel out of control. I turned to alcohol in order to alleviate the stress. Many nights I made it home, not knowing how I made it. My mother stepped in, and helped me raise my two children. Gary was still around arguing with me, and physically abusing me. Drinking alcohol began to be part of my daily ritual. It got to the point where I could not read a tarot card without taking a drink. I was under so much stress.

One day a woman from the local church knocked on the door. "Hello," she yelled, "is anyone here?" I abruptly opened the door, and was surprised to see Sister Creston and Sister Diaz. "Sabrina, I was praying to the Lord about you and I didn't like what he showed me. Are you in need of help? We haven't seen you in church for a long time." As Sister Creston finished her sentence, she glanced around the living room and said, "In the name of Jesus, I cast down these idols." Sister Creston and Sister Diaz began to tear down my altar and removed all of my statues from the house.

I began to cry and fell on my knees. "Help, I need help, they're going to get me," I screamed.

Sister Creston and Sister Diaz began praying and speaking in a foreign tongue. After the two sisters finished praying for me, they decided to talk to me. "Sabrina, I know that you grew up in the church, but something happened. If you want to be saved, repeat the sinner's prayer." Gary wasn't home, so I felt safe enough to speak.

"Sabrina, repeat after me. Dear Jesus, I admit that I am a sinner. Please forgive me for my sins. I believe that you died on the cross for the remission of my sins." I excitedly repeated the sinner's prayer.

"Now," exclaimed Sister Diaz, "you have been forgiven. We will be praying for you," she stated as Sister Creston lifted the heavy bag containing the idols. "Try to make your way to church. Remember, Jesus loves you, and so do I." As I closed the door, I felt a sense of peace. The apartment appeared strange without all of my statues and my altar present.

I began to feel nervous, as if someone were always watching me. I was afraid to stay home alone, when Gary left the apartment in order to go to work. I found no peace at home, so I felt the need to run. I ran to the bars looking for peace. I slowly began to lose everything. All of my clothes were slowly disappearing. Gary went into a rage and cut up most of my clothes with a knife. I owned one pair of shoes and one bra. All of my jewelry was gone. All of my friends were gone. Most of my family turned their backs on me. My enemies began to get the best of me. My husband Gary became even more abusive. My best friend Sheba ran away from me, as if I had a terrible contagious disease. It was difficult to sleep at night. Whenever I tried to go to sleep at night, it felt as if someone, or something, were having sexual intercourse with me, but nobody was there. I tried to comfort myself with alcohol. I began to feel as if I were hallucinating. I seldom felt as if someone were holding me down in my sleep, whenever I did go to sleep. I was tired all of the time. My eyes had the appearance of constant bulging from my face, as if someone were chocking me. At times I would stay in my bed for weeks at a time. There were also times when I closed my eyes, that I literally saw dark-figured men wearing black hoods digging graves at a graveyard scene.

In the midst of my spiritual sickness, I managed to get an order of protection against Gary, which prevented him from coming back into the house. Since I was not working at the time, I was forced to apply for public assistance. This was the first time in my life that I ever had to do this. I was very depressed, and desperate for a breakthrough. I was treated as if I had no education or employment history. I was forced to work at job locations where I was overqualified and underpaid. I was the very song of the drunkards. I dreaded going to the mall, because it was painful for me to see all of the pretty colors printed on the dresses and blouses. Besides, I had no money. I was at the lowest point of my life. I was slowly beginning to lose my memory. I could not remember major events of high school, nor college years. My mind had regressed to the mind of a seventeen year old girl. I became insecure about everything concerning myself and my future.

During my battle to stay alive, my mother agreed to allow Rebecca to stay with her. Gary Jr. stayed with me, while I tried to avoid the fiery flames from the burning missiles that were slowly destroying my life. The rent was past due, and it was beginning to become difficult to buy food and clothes for Gary Jr. and me. The marshal was scheduled to come in at any time, in order to evict us.

One Monday evening I was relaxing in my apartment. Gary Jr. had spent the night at his best friend Ricky's house. I was feeling a little depressed at the time, and began drinking some wine. By the time I had finished, I began to feel even more depressed, and wondered why all of these things were happening to me. The pressure of being a single parent, with few resources or friends, began to overwhelm me. The voices in my head, telling me to come back to the readers for guidance, made me nervous.

81

Although I had refused to continue to work in the kingdom of Satan, I was still being harassed by the demons. All of the areas of my life became engulfed with a fire of hopelessness, which refused to release me. The saints from the church where I was baptized when I was a teenager never came and asked if I needed anything, or if I wanted them to pray for me. The more that I became engulfed in this dangerous fire, the more distant the saints became. It was as if they already declared me as being non-existent. Many days passed by. I felt as if I were existing, but I was not living my life. I was tired of running out of my apartment. I was tired of running out into nothingness. I was tired of running into the bars, searching for freedom. I was tired of not having any money. I was tired of existing.

One evening I was sitting in my empty apartment all alone. There were two twin beds, one for myself and one for Gary jr . The small amount of belongings that Gary jr and I had were stored all around the room in thick, black trash bags. I decided that the bottle of wine that I had in my presence was my best friend. It was there when I needed it. It made me comfortable when I was feeling uneasy and anxious. Anything that I said, it agreed. As I poured the fifth glass of wine, I heard a voice. The voice said, "Go for a walk into the mall across the street. There is a man that you will meet who can help you." I didn't recognize the voice, but I was willing to take a chance and obey. I was desperate to find help. I was desperate to get out of the fire.

As I walked downstairs, already feeling tipsy from the wine that I was drinking previously, I managed to avoid tripping. I entered into the mall with great expectations. Who could this man be? Is there really someone who could really help me with all of these problems? I sat down in the main entrance and waited. Ironically, I met three men, one after the other, who gave me their phone numbers. I was not interested. I knew that not one of them were who I was sent to meet. After sitting down for about forty minutes, a young man walked up to me. He was accompanied by a young woman. She appeared to be overly-protective of him. I pretended as if I didn't see him, but the power of his presence forced me to make eye contact with him. It was him. This was the person that I was sent to meet. I was confident that he could help me. He walked closer to me, and the young lady stood behind him.

"Hi," I stated as he put the shopping bag down beside him. "I know you from the Stapleton area of Staten Island. I grew up there. You look familiar."

"Oh, yes," he replied. "I know you from Stapleton. I grew up there also. What's your name?"

"Sabrina."

"Oh, yeah, Sabrina," he hastily replied. "Your face looks familiar, too." The woman who was walking with him realized that he was safe while speaking with me. She slowly walked away. He was a fair-skinned black man, and was built slightly. He had a gleam in his eyes which told me that he could help me. He was dressed in casual clothes, and had brown curly hair. "Here's my number; my name is Tanus."

"Okay," I replied, "this is my number," I stated as I handed him my home telephone number. "Call me. I have some things that I would like to share with you, Tanus."

"Okay, I will call you as soon as I get a chance, some time tonight."

"Okay, I will speak to you later."

I did not understand why this was all happening, but I was glad that I had someone to talk to. I was satisfied that I had met Tanus, and the purpose for my going to the mall was accomplished. As I entered my apartment, I felt a sigh of relief. It was not even fifteen minutes that I was home in my apartment when the phone rang.

"Hi, Sabrina, this is Tanus."

"Oh, hi, this is Sabrina." As I finished my sentence, I heard the voices in my head telling me to hang up the phone. They told me not to talk to Tanus. I abruptly hung up the phone. Two minutes later the phone rang again. I picked it up, and hung it up without saying a word. The phone rang again. This time I decided to answer the phone.

"Hello."

"Sabrina, it's Tanus. Why do you keep hanging up the phone on me every time that I call you?"

"Oh, I'm sorry," I exclaimed. "I think that I am having problems with my phone. I'm not hanging up on you." I was clearly telling a lie. There were no problems with my phone. I knew that Tanus could help me, and so did the demons.

"Sabrina, when I'm finished over here, I will call you." I began to wonder what this was all about. Even though I just met Tanus, I felt a connection. I believed that I could talk to him about everything that was happening to me, and around me. On the next day, Tanus called me. Since my phone hardly rang, I knew that it was him.

"Sabrina, I know that you told me that you have some things to talk to me about. Why don't you come over to my house and talk?"

"Okay, what's your address? I will take a cab."

"416 Jeroleum Place. I will wait for you," replied Tanus.

As the cab drove up to the white house, I began to feel nervous. I began to reassure myself that Tanus would understand me, and be able to help me. As I entered into the house, he pulled a chair out of the closet for me to sit on.

"So, Sabrina, what is on your mind?"

I began to feel as if I were in the psychologist's chair. I felt very comfortable. I was willing to take a chance, and "spill all of the beans" about my issues. "Well, Tanus, I'm going through a lot of problems.

Something is happening to me. I lost everything, and my son and I are about to be evicted from our apartment. I don't have much money."

"I know that God can help you, Sabrina. It doesn't matter what you're going through, He will help you."

"I forgot to tell you that I used to be a reader. I was involved in rituals using pigeons, and chickens as sacrifices," I confessed. "I used to read tarot cards and tell fortunes. It seems as if ever since I allowed two sisters from the church to tear down my altar and discard my idols, I've been experiencing more problems."

"Don't tell me," replied Tanus. "You gave up your service to the demons, and now they're harassing you. They took everything that you have, right?"

Wow, Tanus was speaking the same language. I felt as if he were the only individual who understood me. Tanus began to read the Bible to me. He took time out of his schedule in order to pray with me and study scripture from the Bible. On the nights that I could not sleep as a result of being harassed by the demons, Tanus stayed up on the phone with me praying and reading the Bible. There were times when Tanus would take me to the movies, and also out to eat dinner. I began to regain some of my memory that I lost. I began to learn more about my creator, Jesus Christ. The more time that I spent with Tanus reading the Bible and praying, I began to feel more alive. I started appreciating the colors of the rainbow. Going to the mall seeing colors on clothing didn't bother me anymore. I was spiritually waking up. Tanus was the first person that I saw when I awoke, spiritually. We began to spend a lot of time together, enjoying each other's company. Over a period of twelve months, Tanus opened up my understanding of why I had to face the obstacles that I was up against. I began to have Bible study with Tanus, and learned powerful Bible principles. Most of all, I learned how to apply these principles. I finally felt strong enough to gain full-time employment. The voice of the Lord divided the flames of the fire.

Although Gary Jr. and I got kicked out of our apartment, I was able to rent a small room for five hundred dollars a month. I was starting to feel more confident about myself. The more that I was reintroduced to my creator, Jesus Christ, the more clarity I received in my daily walk. I started to fall in love with Tanus. I loved him for taking the time to hear my story and help me fight the demons. As time passed by, Tanus and I realized that God did not send him into my life in order to be in a relationship. God, who is almighty, may use anyone or anything in order to accomplish his divine purpose. Our plans may not be what his will is for our lives. Once I fully rededicated my life to Jesus Christ, the demons stopped harassing me. All that I lost, Christ began to give it back. After I was delivered, I learned how to walk in freedom.

One Sunday morning I decided to visit my home church. As I stepped into the church, I heard the choir singing the song that I used to lead, as a teen-ager, *Try Me One More Time*. "Try me one more time. One more time. Give me a chance to know you. Try me one more time. Give me a chance to show you. I will live holy, like you want me to, if you try me one more time." Tears began to fill my eyes.

As the choir members noticed me coming into the sanctuary, they all ran up to me and embraced me. The choir director gave me the microphone. She wanted the Sabrina Matheson who was snatched from the fire to declare that Jesus Christ is Lord, before the congregation. I took the mike, and screamed, "Jesus Christ is Lord." I proceeded to lead the choir, singing *Try Me One More Time*.

> Try me one more time, Lord
> Give me a chance just to know you,
> Try me one more time, Lord
> Give me a chance to show you.

I will live holy, like you want me to,

If you try me one more time. . . .

Only the love of Christ can move true Christians to allow themselves to be used by Christ in order to free the captives and snatch other souls from the fire. The fire is real, the fire is dangerous, but Jesus Christ, the almighty, is all powerful.

Printed in the United States
130890LV00017B/29/A